THE Bezos Letters

Endorsements

"Having served as a 'behind the scenes' executive for most of my career, so much of what Steve Anderson has uncovered about Jeff Bezos and Amazon reminds me of the legacy of Walt Disney. Walt had a vision and made it happen; Jeff had a vision and made it happen; and you too can make your vision happen—and make it happen faster and easier when using the principles Steve has laid out in *The Bezos Letters*. I think there's quite of bit of 'magic' in this book! Great job, Steve!"

Lee Cockerell
Former Executive Vice President of Operations,
WALT DISNEY WORLD® Resort
Bestselling Author of *Creating Magic: Common Sense
Leadership Strategies from a Life at Disney*

"I was just recently in Europe, and I woke up in the middle of the night because of the time difference. I grabbed my iPad and started reading *The Bezos Letters*. I could not put it down. I envision this becoming a college textbook! A roadmap that all young people need to embrace; there are many insights and nuggets for all ages! Well done, Steve. I'll be recommending this book for a long time."

Jim Hackbarth
President and CEO, Assurex Global

"It's easy to think successful businesses have secrets that are protected from the rest of us. But here Steve Anderson has taken the publicly shared Letters to Shareholders and extracted the core principles for all of us to see. There is no Wizard hiding behind a curtain; Jeff Bezos reveals his thinking and strategy from the very beginning of Amazon to the present. If you ever wanted one manual for building and growing your business, this is it."

Dan Miller
New York Times Bestselling Author of
48 Days to the Work You Love

"In a world filled with success hype, this book shines with credibility and authenticity. Each of these letters contains principles that are the result of years of courageous testing, lessons learned through failure, and discoveries that have led to what Amazon is today. If you are growing a business, this is your operations manual. It should be reviewed over and over. If you're not growing a business, these 14 practical principles are the foundation for being the best at whatever you want to be. This is a book I will be giving to my friends."

Ken Davis
Bestselling Author of *Fully Alive*

"As Steve Anderson astutely identifies, Jeff Bezos intentionally embraces experimentation to help him figure out fast what to say Yes to and what to say No to. Such testing can help anyone focus on what really matters. Simply put: *The Bezos Letters* is essential reading."

Greg McKeown
New York Times Bestselling Author of
Essentialism: The Disciplined Pursuit of Less

"My daddy used to say, 'When things are going bad, when your back is against it, you make better decisions because you don't have choices. It's when things are going good that you mess things up because you have too many choices.' Steve Anderson's analysis and understanding of the Bezos / Amazon use of 'successful failure' gives lie to this saying. Steve shows how Amazon consistently makes great decisions when things are going well even though they are in the enviable position of having an almost endless number of choices. Fantastic book. Fantastic analysis."

Duke Williams
Founder, Simply Easier Payments, Inc.

"Anderson takes what is hidden in plain sight, distills down the most important and consistent patterns of Amazon, and shares them in *The Bezos Letters*. The research of each of these letters has led to not just informative stories about the company, although interesting, but highly effective principles that caused such massive growth of Amazon. A fascinating read filled with insights to become like Amazon—Agile, Fast, and Great."

Stephen Roney
Co-Founder and CEO, Roney Innovation
(a top 5% Amazon seller)

"Whether you're a multibillion-dollar tech giant or a small, family-run company, in today's business landscape, staying where you are is falling behind. With *The Bezos Letters*, Steve Anderson offers his own special brand of insight into how Amazon has kept moving forward to become one of the defining business success stories in modern history. Steve's examination of Amazon's core principles is practical, enthralling, and essential for anyone—personally or professionally—and especially the entrepreneur who aspires to seize new opportunities and climb to new heights."

Amy Zupon
CEO, Vertafore

"What if Jeff Bezos simply handed you the formula to Amazon's stratospheric growth so you could do the same? He did, in his shareholder letters. In this remarkable book, Steve Anderson decrypts the 14 Growth Principles you can use to have your own 'Amazon-ing' success!"

Mike Michalowicz
Bestselling Author of *Profit First* and *Clockwork*

"In *The Bezos Letters*, Steve Anderson gives us a deep look into the mind and machinations of the most successful businessperson in history. Using the 14 Growth Principles that Steve identifies from Bezos' Letters to Shareholders, anyone can simplify and streamline explosive business growth."

Chris Tuff
USA Today Bestselling Author of *The Millennial Whisperer*

"Are you a risk taker? I confess at times I've held back wondering, 'What if…?' That's why I love Anderson's approach. He takes the scary out of risk by giving us a plan and a parachute by looking at the ways Jeff Bezos has grown from taking risks, even when the 'what ifs' may have held him back. So, if the risk doesn't bring about change we expected, it may shine a brighter light on better possibilities: whether it's for building a business, expanding an outreach, or enhancing a life. This book is full of rewards for those willing to dream a bigger story."

Patsy Clairmont
Creativity Coach
Bestselling Author of *You Are More Than You Know*

"Why is growing a business so complicated when there are proven strategies right in front of us? Steve Anderson's intelligent, concise, and incredibly well-researched book examines the principles of business success—straight from the most effective risk-taker of our time. If you want to make smarter decisions and earn more money, get your copy of *The Bezos Letters* and start reading. I couldn't put it down."

Janet Switzer
New York Times Bestselling Coauthor with Jack Canfield
The Success Principles: How to Get from Where You Are to Where You Want to Be

"In this informative and engaging work, Steve Anderson takes us on a fascinating journey through CEO Jeff Bezos' letters to uncover the principles and practices that made possible Amazon's meteoric rise from online bookseller to corporate juggernaut. A must read!"

Ian Morgan Cron
Bestselling Author of *The Road Back to You*

"As a direct response marketer for almost forty years, I know how vitally important it is to add value in all we offer, and Amazon has been at the forefront of adding value since Bezos first opened his online bookstore in the '90s. Now, Steve Anderson has added immeasurable value for all of us by uncovering what has made Amazon so successful through the 14 Growth Principles.

"I believe what is revealed in *The Bezos Letters* truly has the potential to change the world for the better. Thank you, Steve. What a gift!"

Brian Kurtz
Titans Marketing
Former Business Builder at Boardroom Inc.
Bestselling Author of *Overdeliver*

"Your Business World is a 3D Movie. Now You'll Have the ONLY Pair of Glasses to See All its Opportunities... Few business books set your mind thinking on a whole new trajectory and far-heightened strata of what's really possible. Nor do many authors provide clear-cut interpretation and penetrating actionable analysis of how a true business-building genius actually sees the future and manifests command and control of all that it makes possible.

"Steve Anderson has taken the rare (yet disarmingly obvious) path of analyzing, deeply interpreting, and then painstakingly analogizing each one of Jeff Bezos' annual shareholder letters. He's figured out the universal code of business 'hyper-growth' that Bezos clearly teaches anyone in business how to master, if they see them.

"Steve's ability to deeply decipher, then break open Bezos' code, lets you gain a 360-degree interpretation and complete translation of how Bezos built every stage of Amazon. He reveals why he chose the strategic processes, paths, and timelines he followed. Steve then shows every business reader how to literally adapt and adopt Amazonian-style growth hormones to whatever you do.

"Steve's super logical approach and amazing ability to interpret, define, and then explain the true meaning of Bezos' statements and subsequent actions are thrilling. I've seen nothing remotely this connective and executable in any business book or autobiography/biography I've ever read.

"In case it's unclear, I am unhedgingly (and passionately) endorsing this book to everyone in business who wants to be more than an incremental performer."

Jay Abraham
World-Renowned Business Strategist
Bestselling Author of *Getting Everything You Can*
Out of All You've Got

The

Bezos Letters

14 Principles to
Grow Your Business
Like Amazon

Steve Anderson

NEW YORK

LONDON • NASHVILLE • MELBOURNE • VANCOUVER

The Bezos Letters
14 Principles to Grow Your Business Like Amazon

© 2020 **Steve Anderson**

Published in New York, New York, by Morgan James Publishing. Morgan James is a trademark of Morgan James, LLC. www.MorganJamesPublishing.com

ISBN 978-1-64279-332-1   paperback
ISBN 978-1-64279-333-8   eBook
ISBN 978-1-64279-675-9   audiobook
Library of Congress Control Number: 2018913098

Cover Design by:
Christos DeVaris

Interior Design by:
Chris Treccani
www.3dogcreative.net

Icon Graphic Design by:
Easel.ly
www.easel.ly

Morgan James is a proud partner of Habitat for Humanity Peninsula and Greater Williamsburg. Partners in building since 2006.

Get involved today! Visit
www.MorganJamesBuilds.com

Dedication

For Karen,
my high school sweetheart, my wife, my friend.
This book would not have happened without you.
Thank you for believing in me!

Note from the Publisher

"Only a few books in history garner the attention organically to become something really special–something business leaders react to and change their course of direction. As a book publisher, we know the power of those books and how those books can change the world. Jeff Bezos was able to see into the future and get products into people's hands globally in ways never before imagined. Now, we are proud to be the publisher of another one of those books. *The Bezos Letters* will help businesses worldwide grow and continue to spread ideas and services that help shape and improve the world like Jeff Bezos does. Well done, Steve!"

David L. Hancock
Founder, Morgan James Publishing

Table of Contents

Foreword

When people ask me what's the one thing they need to make immediate gains in their business, I say, "Get a coach." For the last twenty years—as former chairman and CEO of a $250 million publishing business, and now as the founder and CEO of my own leadership development firm—I've made sure to work with the best and brightest to help me get breakthrough results, personally and professionally.

Through coaching, I've tapped into the wisdom, insight, and experience of others. My coaches have shared what they've learned from their success and—usually better—their failures. And they've given me a different perspective when I couldn't see past my own assumptions and limitations. Their wisdom and insight helped me navigate business in times good, bad, and great. In fact, I can say without a doubt I've gone further and faster than I ever could on my own, thanks to my coaches.

What makes a good coach? Someone who's gone further than you, seen more than you've seen, failed in more interesting ways than you have, and prevailed in the face of challenges more daunting than you've faced. Many people fill that bill, but on the current scene, one especially stands out.

Imagine having Amazon founder and CEO Jeff Bezos as your business coach. I'd jump at that chance, the chance to ask him the not-so-simple question, "How exactly did you grow Amazon?" And I'd love the opportunity to bring his insights and experiences to bear on building and scaling my own business. Who wouldn't?

Unfortunately, that's probably not going to happen for you or me. But fortunately, in *The Bezos Letters*, my friend Steve Anderson has provided the next best thing. Reading *The Bezos Letters* is like having Bezos as your business coach. You get to see what he sees, think what he's thinking, and then apply that to your own business in ways you may never have thought of before—ways Bezos has used to make Amazon one of the world's most successful companies.

How does Steve do that? He's combed through Bezos' letters to Amazon shareholders and identified 14 growth principles. Some of these concepts are obvious in the letters and some lie just under the surface. But Steve shows how they operate together to help Amazon scale unlike any other company. These insights were hiding in plain sight, but I think only Steve would have seen them the way he did.

Steve has spent decades researching and analyzing trends in business and technology, especially focused on risk, and his take is different from what most of us might at first assume. He's kept his finger on the pulse of what's on the horizon and how you can use future opportunities to your advantage.

Think of him as your guide to the mind of Jeff Bezos. He's like an archeologist, working deep in the—forgive the pun—Amazon, having found a remarkable structure that few have been able to understand or whose inscriptions few have deciphered. But Steve has decoded the logic behind the Bezos letters for all of us and translated it into language that's simultaneously easy to grasp and apply in almost every business or organization.

Beyond that, Steve has provided fascinating stories on everything from how Bezos has experienced "successful failure" to how Bezos looks at space. These stories become windows into ways we can all grow in the future.

With Bezos as your coach and Steve as your translator, you'll clearly see how to take your business to a higher, more productive, more impactful level. When you apply Steve's 14 Growth Principles revealed in *The Bezos Letters* to your business, you'll have everything you need to grow your business like Amazon.

Michael Hyatt
CEO, Michael Hyatt & Company
New York Times Bestselling Author,
Free to Focus and *Your Best Year Ever*

Risk and Growth

After thirty-five-plus years of studying the business side of risk, I believe there are really only two kinds: risks of commission and risks of omission. In other words, risks you take and risks you don't take.

Due to Jeff Bezos, Amazon is the fastest company in history to reach $100 billion in sales.

So, how did he do it?

Jeff Bezos is, arguably, the master of risk.

***

Having spent most of my career as a speaker and consultant on technology and risk, I know that many people think it's always important to be protected *from* risk. Risk is viewed as inherently "bad," and people do what they can to make sure they are covered if something unforeseen and devastating should happen, leaving them vulnerable and financially exposed.

Except, I don't look at risk that way... and, I discovered, neither does Jeff Bezos.

What I've come to realize is there is an essential link between risk and business growth that many people overlook. From this vantage point, risk can be framed in a very positive light. That's why this book is looking at the growth of Amazon from a slightly different perspective—through the lens of risk.

Yes, every business takes risks, but haphazard risk-taking is like rolling the dice. You never know what's going to come up. But Bezos takes risks with *intentionality*, which most businesses, if aware, can also harness to achieve greater results.

I believe what has fueled Amazon's growth comes down to Jeff Bezos' unique approach to taking and leveraging risk and his commitment to creating a culture for experimentation and invention. And it's all based on his views on success and, actually, failure.

The Beginning

In July 1994, thirty-year-old Jeff Bezos started a little online bookstore called Amazon.com, named after the longest river in South America. (Interestingly, Amazon.com was very nearly called "Cadabra," as in "abracadabra." Bezos decided to change the name when his lawyer misheard the word as "cadaver.")

Amazon was instead named after the river reportedly for two reasons. One, to suggest scale (Amazon.com launched with the tagline "Earth's Biggest Bookstore") and two, back then websites were often listed in alphabetical order and Amazon would show up first.

What started as a simple idea would quickly grow into one of the most valuable companies in the world (based on market capitalization) along with Apple, Microsoft, and Google. Amazon is the fastest company ever to reach $100 billion in sales. It was one of the first companies to be valued at $1 trillion. It employs over 647,000 people, a number greater than the population of many countries, including Luxembourg, Iceland, and the Bahamas. In 2010 Bezos said,

> "I got the idea to start Amazon 16 years ago. I came across the fact that Web usage was growing at 2,300 percent per year. I'd never seen or heard of anything that grew that fast, and the idea of building an online

bookstore with millions of titles—something that simply couldn't exist in the physical world—was very exciting to me.

"I had just turned 30 years old, and I'd been married for a year. I told my wife, MacKenzie, that I wanted to quit my job and go do this crazy thing that probably wouldn't work since most startups don't, and I wasn't sure what would happen after that. MacKenzie (also a Princeton grad and sitting here in the second row) told me I should go for it.

"As a young boy, I'd been a garage inventor. I'd invented an automatic gate closer out of cement-filled tires, a solar cooker that didn't work very well out of an umbrella and tinfoil, baking-pan alarms to entrap my siblings. I'd always wanted to be an inventor, and she wanted me to follow my passion." —2010 Princeton University Baccalaureate Speech[1]

During its first twenty years in business, Amazon survived the dot-com bubble of the early 2000s, the Financial Crisis and Great Recession from 2007–2009, and countless other financial crises that took out many of Amazon's contemporaries.

By the time Amazon hit its $1 trillion valuation in 2018, Bezos had surpassed Bill Gates, Warren Buffett, and seven billion other people to become the wealthiest person in the world, with a net worth of $137 billion (give or take).

What propelled this unprecedented growth?

And how did Bezos build an online bookstore into a trillion-dollar company during a period that saw countless other technology companies and bookstores collapse? What would you give to have Bezos himself explain the secrets that took Amazon to a trillion-dollar company and him to become the wealthiest person in the world?

Fortunately, Bezos didn't operate behind a curtain, hiding his mechanisms and strategies like the Wizard of Oz. That's where the

Shareholder Letters come in. They reveal his thinking and his strategy from the beginning of Amazon to the present.

Bezos was extremely savvy when it came to growing Amazon: he knew there was an exquisite tension between risk and growth. *You don't grow if you're not willing to take risks.*

But here's where Bezos does what I consider to be incredibly astute: he chooses to play the game differently by always assessing his "return on risk."

"Return on Risk," or ROR, is a term I use to refer to the relationship between the cost of risk and its return (which isn't always financial). It's similar to how you would think of a "Return on Investment," or ROI.

"Return on Risk"

From the owner to the receptionist, everyone in business understands that everything we do has a cost and a benefit. Every dollar we spend to advertise, pay salary, buy materials, deliver goods, build a website, and anything else we do, should create more than a dollar in return. Every minute we spend working on something should similarly create an income worthy of the time spent.

Although most everyone in business views money spent on the business through an investment framework, virtually no one thinks about business risk as an investment—with the possible exception of Jeff Bezos.

When the internet was first launching into the mainstream, Bezos was quick to observe that a 2300 percent growth rate was exceptional. He quit his stable Wall Street job to launch an online business when most of the online businesses at the time were of "questionable repute." He got a $300K loan from his parents and moved his family across the country to start an unknown business.

Was that risky? I'd say so.

Remember, as Amazon was starting out, Jeff Bezos was launching an online bookstore. *Nobody knew what an online bookstore was.*

In 1997, most people didn't have internet access at home, and if they did, it was "dial-up" (remember the movie *You've Got Mail?*). In fact, in his '97 Letter, Bezos referred to the internet as the "World Wide Wait."

Here's a picture of what 1997 was like when Bezos was first starting Amazon: The first Harry Potter book, *Harry Potter and the Philosopher's Stone* by (now billionaire) J.K. Rowling had just come out in the UK. There were no other Harry Potter books, movies, or theme parks, just a Harry Potter book for kids to read.

The year 1997 also brought us Bill Clinton, *Friends*, *Titanic*, and Beanie Babies; there was no such thing as "cloud computing" (clouds were still up in the big blue sky). Netscape was the browser of choice for those who had internet access, and DVDs were just coming of age because live streaming was still twenty years in the future.

And Bezos *quit his job* to start an online bookstore.

Bezos certainly took a risk for his online business at a time that an online business was a crap shoot, at best. Just a short year after Amazon went public, Bezos wrote:

"We predict the next 3½ years will be even more exciting. We are working to build a place where tens of millions of customers can come to find and discover anything they might want to buy online. It is truly Day 1 for the Internet and, if we execute our business plan well, it remains Day 1 for Amazon.com. Given what's happened, it may be difficult to conceive, but we think the opportunities and risks ahead of us are even greater than those behind us. We will have to make many conscious and deliberate choices, some of which will be bold and unconventional. Hopefully, some

will turn out to be winners. Certainly, some will turn out to be mistakes."
—Bezos (1998 Letter)

In hindsight, Bezos did have a few "mistakes," but he also had unprecedented growth.

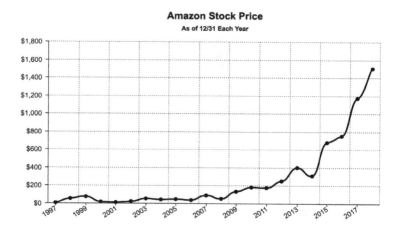

Amazon Stock Price
As of 12/31 Each Year

Suffice it to say, even though he started with a main idea and business model, although it looked like he put "all his eggs in one basket," his plan was diversification from the beginning. The difference is that he was always testing to see what the market wanted and inventing on behalf of the customer, even when they didn't know what they wanted. His risks were intentional and calculated, but still risks, nonetheless.

He started by taking a risk with an idea for a dot-com business and, with the money he would scrape together and with a loan from his parents, he leveraged that idea into Amazon, a company that has gained worldwide recognition and made him the wealthiest man in the world.

And that's why Bezos is such a master of risk.

Why The Bezos Letters?

"...we choose to **prioritize growth** because we believe that scale is central to achieving the potential of our business model." —Bezos (1997 Letter)

A few years ago, I was involved in an industry workgroup investigating the changing nature of risk. I began researching the subject of risk in business when I came across the annual Letters to Shareholders that Jeff Bezos, founder of Amazon, has written for the last twenty-one years.

I've been a student of business, large and small, for the better part of four decades, and I'm always "reading between the lines" to find what makes the difference between success and failure.

As I studied the letters, ideas and patterns began to emerge. I realized Bezos was actually spelling out through his letters how Amazon came to be the fastest growing and, some would say, most successful company the world has ever seen.

Over time, as I analyzed and studied the letters, it became evident to me that there were actually Cycles of Growth and 14 Growth Principles that could help *any* businesses in *any* industry.

And what's more, it was evident you don't need billions of dollars to implement any of the principles. Even Amazon didn't have billions of dollars when they got started (Bezos actually started with a $300K loan from his parents).

Most of the principles don't cost a penny. You could implement them in a business in Silicon Valley, Nashville, London, or Des Moines. You could just as easily apply them to a tech company, a pizza shop, or non-profit organization.

At first, I was somewhat surprised that there were really only 14 growth principles that made Amazon a trillion-dollar company. I diligently looked for more, but everything fit squarely within one or more of the 14 principles.

And, like most ideas that are impactful, the 14 Growth Principles (when you become aware of them) are quite simple—but in no way are they simplistic.

You don't need an advanced degree or a huge team to make any of them happen. In fact, after learning them, I'm confident every business owner can start using these principles right away.

I say that, even without knowing anything about you or your business. In fact, I've been working with public and private companies for decades and I can't think of a single client I've had throughout the years who couldn't start using these principles immediately.

It doesn't matter whether you are a multinational corporation, a solopreneur, or today's equivalent of a start-up online bookstore, the first step to growing your business like Amazon is to start with the fundamentals that Bezos reveals.

From the outset, let me say these are *not* Bezos' or Amazon's stated principles; they are mine—principles I extracted when studying the letters that Bezos wrote to his shareholders documenting Amazon's position and growth in the marketplace.

At first glance, Bezos' letters to shareholders (which I simply call the Shareholder Letters) offer readers an interesting glimpse into one of the world's most successful companies.

But if you dig deeper and read the Shareholder Letters as one narrative rather than twenty-plus independent annual letters, like I said, patterns emerge. And when you read the Shareholder Letters within the context of Amazon's business and what was happening in the world at the time each letter was written, so much more jumps off the pages that can be applied to business today.

I analyzed the twenty-one Shareholder Letters[2] between 1997 and 2018. I looked into what Bezos actually said about how Amazon operated between 1994 and 2018 and what led to Amazon's phenomenal growth. I examined what worked and what didn't work. I read, re-read, researched, and dissected everything about each of the Shareholder Letters to learn how Bezos turned an online bookstore into a trillion-dollar company in just over two decades.

You may ask, did Jeff Bezos start out with these growth principles in mind?

Well, yes and no.

No, because they weren't articulated as such by Bezos. They came from my examination and analysis of his letters. Obviously, he didn't have them spelled out and framed in his office since he didn't write them. What he did have prominently displayed in his office were *Amazon* **Leadership** *Principles* (I've included them in Growth Principle 11). As it states on the Amazon website:

> "Amazon Leadership Principles are a set of standards all Amazonians aspire to every day; they are ingrained in our culture. Employees love them because they clearly explain the kinds of behaviors we value. As an Amazon employee, you'll rarely have a day go by without hearing our Amazon Leadership Principles referenced, as a shorthand for doing the right thing. They are a universal approach to how we work here."[3]

Most people would agree that a company can't grow to its fullest potential without great leadership. Leadership is at the center of business growth and deeply ingrained in the core of Amazon.

Bezos has been intentional, since the beginning of his business, to encourage leadership in every area of Amazon.

But business leadership is different than business *growth*.

So, to answer the question of whether Bezos started out with the growth principles, I believe he did; he just didn't articulate them in a defined way. He didn't spell them out in the same way as the Amazon Leadership Principles, but from the very first letter to shareholders, these 14 Growth Principles I uncovered were at the heart of how Amazon grew. They were *intuitive* to Bezos. They emerged from his personality and business experience.

But just because they were intuitive to him in his business doesn't mean you can't use those same principles to grow your business. To be clear, the purpose of this book is not to have you *become* the next Amazon (although that may happen, and Bezos is actually planning for Amazon's eventual obsolescence, but that's another story).

What I'm suggesting is that you look at how Amazon has grown using the 14 Growth Principles and see what you can apply to your business or organization and expand in a way that positions you at the forefront *like* Amazon.

The Growth Cycles and 14 Principles

Again, as I was studying the Shareholder Letters, I realized they split into repeatable Growth Cycles that Bezos applies to pretty much every endeavor: *test, build, accelerate,* and *scale* with the principles falling into each area.

Three of the principles helped Amazon grow through strategic **testing:**

- Encourage "Successful Failure"
- Bet on Big Ideas
- Practice Dynamic Invention and Innovation

Three of the principles helped Amazon **build** for the future:

- Obsess Over Customers
- Apply Long-Term Thinking
- Understand Your Flywheel

Four of the principles helped Amazon **accelerate** its growth:

- Generate High-Velocity Decisions
- Make Complexity Simple
- Accelerate Time with Technology
- Promote Ownership

And four of the principles helped Amazon **scale:**

- Maintain Your Culture
- Focus on High Standards
- Measure What Matters, Question What's Measured, and Trust Your Gut
- Believe It's Always Day 1

While the terms *test, build, accelerate,* and *scale* are familiar to many business owners, they take on a different meaning within the context of the Shareholder Letters.

If there is one big difference between what test, build, accelerate, and scale mean at Amazon, it's that Amazon doesn't treat those terms as *academic.* They make these cycles a part of their planning process with the same kind of *intentionality* that Bezos pays to risk.

To Bezos, businesses are always changing and moving. Growing businesses are always testing something, building something, accelerating something, and scaling something.

And when you find out what works, you do it all over again.

The First Bezos Letter to Shareholders

Jeff Bezos wrote his first letter to shareholders in 1997. (Each shareholder letter typically comes out in April of the following year. For commentary and analyses of future Shareholder Letters—2019 and beyond—go to TheBezosLetters.com.)

It was "Day 1" for Amazon, referring to all the excitement, commitment to serving customers beyond their expectations, and cutting-edge offerings that fuel the fires of a startup.

But interestingly, the next year when he wrote the 1998 shareholder letter, at the end of the letter he referred back to the '97 Letter. And he did the same in '99, referring back to the original '97 Letter. And the next year, and the next year... and *every year since then*. He always goes back to the original '97 Letter.

As time went by, the closing statement at the end of each Shareholder Letter remained the same, and only became more succinct:

"As always, I attach a copy of our original 1997 letter. It remains Day 1."

Again, as I looked at the twenty-one years of letters as a whole and Amazon's seemingly meteoric growth, I wondered why he kept referring back to that 1997 Letter where he first referenced Day 1.

Three ideas emerged.

First, a central point of the 1997 Letter was Amazon's commitment to focus on the long-term.

Bezos didn't want investors who were only in it for a quick hit. He was focused on the long game. He was creating a company he wanted to be able to tell his grandchildren about... and he didn't even have any grandchildren.

Second, the 1997 Letter communicated his passion for the company and the necessary "startup" elements for making a successful and *sustaining* business—like being obsessed about your customers and constant invention on behalf of customers, just to name a few. These are the elements for business success he affectionately calls "Day 1."

Third, in some way or other, the concept of risk was always present. At the beginning of the '97 Letter, when talking about the future and what it will entail, he says very clearly, "This strategy is not without risk..." He also talks about growth challenges and execution risk as well as the risks of product and geographic expansion. Suffice it to say, growing fast is fraught with risk.

Yet, in the midst of all the growth and risk, Bezos was clear as to his core value: obsessing over customers.

As I said, the Amazon Leadership Principles are an integral part of the Amazon culture. They are not numbered, but they start out with Customer Obsession.[4]

> **"Amazon Leadership Principles—Customer Obsession:** Leaders start with the customer and work backwards. They work vigorously to earn and keep customer trust. Although leaders pay attention to competitors, they obsess over customers."

And you would think that Customer Obsession is where business *growth* would start because business is "always about the customer." However, this is where leadership and business growth start to deviate.

To grow your business, you have to work with the end in mind, but your ultimate "end game" is different than purely focusing on customers.

Simply put, leadership principles focus on *people,* and growth principles focus on the *business as a whole.* Of course, there is overlap—but leadership principles apply to the way people work, and growth principles apply to the way the business or organization works. That's why the list of Growth Principles *end* with Day 1 instead of starting there. To grow your business, you will come full circle.

As I was going through all the Shareholder Letters that Bezos had sent out over the past twenty-one years, I realized something extraordinary.

After I identified the Growth Cycles and 14 Growth Principles that were the essential components for Amazon growing the way it has, I went back and, after further examination, I found that in some form or another, *all 14 Growth Principles appeared in that very first* 1997 Letter to Shareholders. In my mind, this is one of the reasons he keeps referring back to his original letter.

Now you may wonder since I've never worked at Amazon or for Amazon, what makes me qualified to write this book?

Sometimes, an outsider can give perspective that an insider can't. And, in fact, my take on Amazon's growth is through an entirely different lens—that of risk.

You see, I have been a business and risk analyst my whole career. My lens has been through the insurance industry where I've been a technology consultant and futurist helping businesses of all sizes, and from both sides (the company side providing coverage and the consumer side needing protection), to evaluate and "manage" their risks.

That's the mindset I had when I came upon the Shareholder Letters and discovered Bezos has been using risk *strategically*, and to his advantage, for the last twenty-five-plus years.

Unfortunately, most people will not take the time to read all twenty-one years of the Shareholder Letters (although I would highly suggest doing just that as they are extraordinarily insightful). And because many would find reading all the letters "challenging," I'm not including them here. But throughout this book I will be using various quotes and ideas from the letters that demonstrate or support the Growth Cycles and my 14 Growth Principles.

I've painstakingly gone through and pulled out what you need to know. And to make it easier, in the quotes from Bezos at the beginning of the chapters, I have bolded the words that express his core idea so you can quickly find them. (Bezos doesn't use bold in his writings, so any quote with bold you will know is my emphasis.)

And to be clear, each of the 14 Growth Principles operate individually–but *none of the principles operate in isolation.* They're evident in some fashion in everything Amazon has done to build the company it is today.

So, here's how I suggest you read the book to get the most out of it.

- First, familiarize yourself with the Growth Cycles and 14 Growth Principles I have extrapolated from Bezos' letters. That will give you an overview of what's to come.

- Next, take the time to read Jeff Bezos' 1997 Letter to Shareholders. It's the first letter he wrote and the one he refers back to each year. It is the foundational "linchpin" for how he thinks and why he does what he does.

   As you read the '97 Letter, you'll see every time I found one of the 14 Growth Principles *in the letter* I've noted that in **bold.** The Growth Principles are not in any kind of order in the Letter, but you'll see they are all there.

- After that, you'll see I've divided the book into the Growth Cycles with the corresponding Growth Principles. The principles are described in detail with quotes from Bezos, stories of Amazon, and the lessons they learned (and lessons you can learn from) as they started, grew, failed, regrouped, and morphed into what they are today.

- At the end of each chapter, there are two or three short questions. Take a moment to think about your answer. All it takes is one new idea that could lead to massive growth.

- After the chapters about the 14 Growth Principles, I've taken the 2018 Letter to Shareowners and added the principles *in the letter* and the concepts in **bold** just like in the '97 Letter. And, now that you're familiar with the 14 Growth Principles, you'll see, in some way or another, they are all there.

One other thing before we begin. I would hope that as you learn about the Growth Cycles and 14 Growth Principles, you'll start to understand why they were "hidden in plain sight" in the Shareholder Letters. And by the time you get to the end and read the 2018 Letter, you may find the principles in different places than I found them. Nothing could please me more.

Because that's my hope for this book—that you will be able to see through the lens of risk and identify in your own business where you can find the 14 Growth Principles.

Now, is Amazon a "perfect company"? No. Is Jeff Bezos a "perfect man"? No.

You may love Amazon or hate Amazon. You may love Jeff Bezos or hate him. Whatever you feel about Amazon and Bezos is okay.

But for the purpose of this book—and for the benefit of your future business growth—I'm going to ask you to suspend your feelings about Amazon and Bezos and step back and take a 30,000-foot view to see what Bezos (and Amazon) has done to secure its historic role as the fastest growing company in the world to reach $100 billion in sales.

The Anderson 14 Growth Principles

Growth Cycles:
Test, Build, Accelerate, Scale

Test

Principle 1. Encourage "Successful Failure"

Principle 2. Bet on Big Ideas

Principle 3. Practice Dynamic Invention and Innovation

Build

Principle 4. Obsess Over Customers

Principle 5. Apply Long-Term Thinking

Principle 6. Understand Your Flywheel

Accelerate

Principle 7. Generate High-Velocity Decisions

Principle 8. Make Complexity Simple

Principle 9. Accelerate Time with Technology

Principle 10. Promote Ownership

Scale

Principle 11. Maintain Your Culture

Principle 12. Focus on High Standards

Principle 13. Measure What Matters, Question What's Measured, and Trust Your Gut

Principle 14. Believe It's Always Day 1

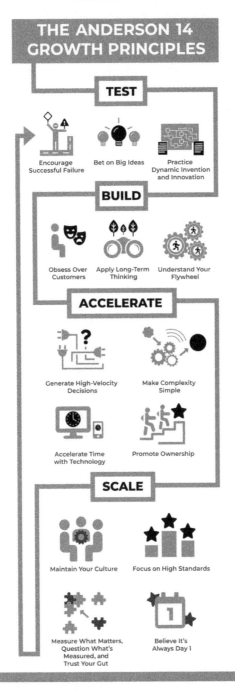

THE ANDERSON 14 GROWTH PRINCIPLES

TEST

Encourage Successful Failure

Bet on Big Ideas

Practice Dynamic Invention and Innovation

BUILD

Obsess Over Customers

Apply Long-Term Thinking

Understand Your Flywheel

ACCELERATE

Generate High-Velocity Decisions

Make Complexity Simple

Accelerate Time with Technology

Promote Ownership

SCALE

Maintain Your Culture

Focus on High Standards

Measure What Matters, Question What's Measured, and Trust Your Gut

Believe It's Always Day 1

1997 Letter to Shareholders with The Anderson 14 Growth Principles (highlighted)

To our shareholders:

Amazon.com passed many milestones in 1997: by year-end, we had served more than 1.5 million customers, yielding 838% revenue growth to $147.8 million, and extended our market leadership despite aggressive competitive entry.

But this is **Day 1** *(14 Believe It's Always Day 1)* for the Internet and, if we execute well, for Amazon.com. Today, online commerce saves customers money and precious time. Tomorrow, through personalization, online commerce will accelerate the very **process of discovery** *(3 Practice Dynamic Invention and Innovation)*. Amazon.com uses the Internet to create real value for its customers and, by doing so, hopes to create an enduring franchise, even in established and large markets.

We have a window of opportunity as larger players marshal the resources to pursue the online opportunity and as customers, new to purchasing online, are receptive to forming new relationships. The competitive landscape has continued to evolve at a fast pace. Many large players have moved online with credible offerings and have devoted substantial energy and resources to building awareness, traffic, and sales. Our goal is to move quickly to solidify and **extend our current position** (2 Bet on Big Ideas) while we begin to pursue the online commerce opportunities in other areas. We see substantial opportunity in the large markets we are targeting. This strategy is not without risk; it requires serious investment and crisp execution against established franchise leaders.

It's All About the Long Term

We believe that a fundamental measure of our success will be the shareholder value we create over the **long term** (5 Apply Long-Term Thinking). This value will be a direct result of our ability to extend and solidify our current market leadership position. The stronger our market leadership, the more powerful our economic model. Market leadership can translate directly to higher revenue, higher profitability, greater capital velocity, and correspondingly stronger returns on invested capital.

Our decisions have consistently reflected this focus. We first **measure** (13 Measure What Matters, Question What's Measured, and Trust Your Gut) ourselves in terms of the metrics most indicative of our market leadership: customer and revenue growth, the degree to which our customers continue to purchase from us on a repeat basis, and the strength of our brand. **We have invested and will continue to invest aggressively to expand and leverage our customer base, brand, and infrastructure as we move to establish an enduring franchise** (6 Understand Your Flywheel).

Because of our emphasis on the long term, we may make decisions and weigh tradeoffs differently than some companies. Accordingly, we want to share with you our fundamental management and **decision-**

making approach (7 Generate High-Velocity Decisions) so that you, our shareholders, may confirm that it is consistent with your investment philosophy:

- We will continue to **focus relentlessly on our customers** (4 Obsess Over Customers).

- We will continue to make investment decisions in light of long-term market leadership considerations rather than short-term profitability considerations or short-term Wall Street reactions.

- We will continue to measure our programs and the effectiveness of our investments analytically, to jettison those that don't provide acceptable returns, and to step up our investment in those that work best. We will continue to **learn from both our successes and our failures** (1 Encourage "Successful Failure").

- We will make bold rather than timid investment decisions where we see a sufficient probability of gaining market leadership advantages. Some of these investments will pay off, others will not, and we will have learned another valuable lesson in either case.

- When forced to choose between optimizing the appearance of our GAAP accounting and maximizing the present value of future cash flows, we'll take the cash flows.

- We will share our strategic thought processes with you when we make bold choices (to the extent competitive pressures allow), so that you may evaluate for yourselves whether we are making rational long-term leadership investments.

- We will work hard to spend wisely and maintain our lean culture. We understand the importance of continually reinforcing a cost-conscious culture, particularly in a business incurring net losses.

- We will balance our focus on growth with emphasis on long-term profitability and capital management. At this stage, we choose to prioritize growth because we believe that scale is central to achieving the potential of our business model.

- We will continue to focus on hiring and retaining versatile and talented employees, and continue to weight their compensation to stock options rather than cash. We know our success will be largely affected by our ability to attract and retain a motivated employee base, each of whom must think like, and therefore must actually **be, an owner** (10 Promote Ownership).

We aren't so bold as to claim that the above is the "right" investment philosophy, but it's ours, and we would be remiss if we weren't clear in the approach we have taken and will continue to take.

With this foundation, we would like to turn to a review of our business focus, our progress in 1997, and our outlook for the future.

Obsess Over Customers

From the beginning, our focus has been on offering our customers compelling value. We realized that the Web was, and still is, the World Wide Wait. Therefore, we set out to offer customers something they simply couldn't get any other way and began serving them with books. We brought them much more selection than was possible in a physical store (our store would now occupy 6 football fields), and presented it in a **useful, easy-to-search, and easy-to-browse format** *(8 Make Complexity Simple)* in a store open **365 days a year, 24 hours a day** *(9 Accelerate Time with Technology).* We maintained a dogged focus on improving the shopping experience, and in 1997 substantially enhanced our store. We now offer customers gift certificates, 1-Click shopping, and vastly more reviews, content, browsing options, and recommendation features. We dramatically lowered prices, further increasing customer value. Word of mouth remains the most powerful customer acquisition tool we have, and we are grateful for the trust our customers have placed in us. Repeat purchases and word of mouth have combined to make Amazon.com the market leader in online bookselling.

By many measures, Amazon.com came a long way in 1997:

- Sales grew from $15.7 million in 1996 to $147.8 million—an 838% increase.

- Cumulative customer accounts grew from 180,000 to 1,510,000—a 738% increase.

- The percentage of orders from repeat customers grew from over 46% in the fourth quarter of 1996 to over 58% in the same period in 1997.

- In terms of audience reach, per Media Metrix, our Web site went from a rank of 90th to within the top 20.

- We established long-term relationships with many important strategic partners, including America Online, Yahoo!, Excite, Netscape, GeoCities, AltaVista, @Home, and Prodigy.

Infrastructure

During 1997, we worked hard to expand our business infrastructure to support these greatly increased traffic, sales, and service levels:

- Amazon.com's employee base grew from 158 to 614, and we significantly strengthened our management team.

- Distribution center capacity grew from 50,000 to 285,000 square feet, including a 70% expansion of our Seattle facilities and the launch of our second distribution center in Delaware in November.

- Inventories rose to over 200,000 titles at year-end, enabling us to improve availability for our customers.

- Our cash and investment balances at year-end were $125 million, thanks to our initial public offering in May 1997 and our $75 million loan, affording us substantial strategic flexibility.

Our Employees

The past year's success is the product of a talented, smart, hard-working group, and I take great pride in being a part of this team. **Setting the bar high** (12 Focus on High Standards) in our approach to hiring has been, and will continue to be, the single most important element of Amazon. com's success.

It's not easy to work here (when I interview people I tell them, "You can work long, hard, or smart, but at Amazon.com you can't choose two out of three"), but we are working to **build something important, something that matters** (11 Maintain Your Culture) to our customers, something that we can all tell our grandchildren about. Such things aren't meant to be easy. We are incredibly fortunate to have this group of dedicated employees whose sacrifices and passion build Amazon. com.

Goals for 1998

We are still in the early stages of learning how to bring new value to our customers through Internet commerce and merchandising. Our goal remains to continue to solidify and extend our brand and customer base. This requires sustained investment in systems and infrastructure to support outstanding customer convenience, selection, and service while we grow. We are planning to add music to our product offering, and over time we believe that other products may be prudent investments. We also believe there are significant opportunities to better serve our customers overseas, such as reducing delivery times and better tailoring the customer experience. To be certain, a big part of the challenge for us will lie not in finding new ways to expand our business, but in prioritizing our investments.

We now know vastly more about online commerce than when Amazon. com was founded, but we still have so much to learn. Though we are optimistic, we must remain vigilant and maintain a sense of urgency. The challenges and hurdles we will face to make our long-term vision for Amazon.com a reality are several: aggressive, capable, well-funded competition; considerable growth challenges and execution risk; the risks of product and geographic expansion; and the need for large continuing investments to meet an expanding market opportunity. However, as we've long said, online bookselling, and online commerce in general, should prove to be a very large market, and it's likely that a number of companies will see significant benefit. We feel good about what we've done, and even more excited about what we want to do.

1997 was indeed an incredible year. We at Amazon.com are grateful to our customers for their business and trust, to each other for our hard work, and to our shareholders for their support and encouragement.

/s/ JEFFREY P. BEZOS
Jeffrey P. Bezos
Founder and Chief Executive Officer
Amazon.com, Inc.

Growth Cycle: Test

Encourage Successful Failure

Bet on Big Ideas

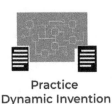

Practice Dynamic Invention and Innovation

At Amazon, testing is a way of life; it means encouraging all team members to try new things to improve the way Amazon does business. If something doesn't work, they aren't punished—they are encouraged to examine what didn't work and *learn* from it.

When something works and has big potential, Amazon bets big. They give everyone the tools to be inventive at every level. Testing makes Amazon an extremely creative organization.

But testing, by definition, requires risking failure. Most businesses view failure as a risk to be avoided. Bezos thinks the exact opposite.

Chapter One

Principle 1: Encourage "Successful Failure"

"I've made billions of dollars of failures at Amazon.com. Literally billions of dollars of failures. You might remember Pets.com or Kosmo.com. It was like getting a root canal with no anesthesia. None of those things are fun. **But they also don't matter**." —2014 *Business Insider* IGNITION conference[5]

Why in the world would Bezos say that blowing billions of dollars doesn't matter?

The answer to that question is actually how he made those billions of dollars *in the first place*.

Jeff Bezos figured out very early on that unless you take risks, invest in risks, and intentionally create opportunities for "failure," you're not growing or thinking big enough.

Unfortunately, most people (and businesses) think of failure as something to be avoided at all costs. However, you'll never be able to grow like Amazon if you're not willing to risk failure.

But if failure isn't always a bad thing, then what makes failure... "successful"?

In short, successful failure is what you *learn* from failure and how you apply what you've learned, and that makes all the difference.

Risk and Space

I believe Jeff Bezos has been thinking about risk since he was a little kid and fell in love with outer space. It may initially seem unrelated to how Amazon has grown, but it speaks to who Jeff Bezos is and why he thinks the way he does.

Bezos was born in 1964 in the dawn of America's space exploration. In his high school valedictorian speech, he talked about space travel and exploration, and he's been obsessed with aerospace from as far back as I can trace. (More on his space connection later.)

Two events occurred in the NASA (National Aeronautics and Space Administration) program Apollo during Bezos' childhood that demonstrate the concept of failure and "successful failure." In fact, the lessons from these two events represent Bezos' way of thinking about risk better than anything I've found.

Let's start back in the beginning days of NASA.

In the early 1960s, NASA created the Mercury, Gemini, and Apollo projects with the ultimate goal to land humans on the Moon and bring them safely back to Earth.

But the first attempt, Apollo 1, was a heartbreaking tragedy.

On January 27, 1967, a flash fire erupted during preflight testing at Cape Canaveral. That intense fire swept through the command module, killing commander Virgil "Gus" Grissom, Ed White, and Roger Chaffee.

Immediately after the fire, NASA convened an Accident Review Board to determine the cause of the accident. It was determined that the fire was electrical and spread rapidly due to combustible nylon material and the high-pressure, pure-oxygen cabin atmosphere.

Further, the astronauts' rescue was impeded because the door hatch couldn't be opened due to the higher internal pressure of the cabin. Additionally, the preflight test wasn't deemed "hazardous" since the rocket was unfueled. The rescue was also hampered by poor emergency preparedness.

It was later determined that the astronauts died from asphyxiation when the module filled with toxic gas, smoke, and fire.

The world was rocked with grief.

Even though NASA and all the astronauts were well aware of the risks of what could happen when attempting something that had never been done before, there were still the "what ifs." Many wondered if the quest to land on the Moon was over. The cost seemed pretty high.

The disaster of Apollo 1 shook NASA to its core.

In the documentary *Mission Control: The Unsung Heroes of Apollo,* the horrifying tragedy was recounted in detail. Chris Kraft was Director of Flight Operations and Gene Kranz was Flight Director.

On Monday morning after the tragedy, Kranz called a meeting of the flight control team and included civil servants, controllers, and spacecraft contractors. They were all deeply disturbed by the fire and still searching for answers.

The meeting began by citing the known facts of the accident, then describing the newly appointed Review Board and the investigating team headed by the director of the Langley Research Center, Floyd Thompson.

Kranz later said his feelings had gone from shock to one of pure anger—anger that in some way Flight Control had let the crew down.

He began by saying that they were all responsible for killing the crew, that they had not done their jobs.

Kranz began what is now known as "The Kranz Dictum":[6]

"Spaceflight will never tolerate carelessness, incapacity, and neglect. Somewhere, somehow, we screwed up. It could have been in design, build, or test. Whatever it was, we should have caught it.

"We were too gung-ho about the schedule, and we locked out all of the problems we saw each day in our work. Every element of the program was in trouble and so were we. The simulators were not working, Mission Control was behind in virtually every area, and the flight and test procedures changed daily. Nothing we did had any shelf life. Not one of us stood up and said, 'Dammit, stop!'

"I don't know what Thompson's committee will find as the cause, but I know what I find. We are the cause! We were not ready! We didn't do our job.

"We were rolling the dice, hoping that things would come together by launch day, when in our hearts we knew it would take a miracle. We were pushing the schedule and betting that the Cape would slip before we did.

"From this day forward, Flight Control will be known by two words: *Tough* and *Competent*.

"*Tough* means we are forever accountable for what we do or what we fail to do. We will never again compromise our responsibilities. Every time we walk into Mission Control we will know what we stand for.

"*Competent* means we will never take anything for granted. We will never be found short in our knowledge and in our skills. Mission Control will be perfect.

"When you leave this meeting today, you will go to your office and the first thing you will do there is to write 'Tough and Competent' on your blackboards. It will never be erased. Each day when you enter the room, these words will remind you of the price paid by Grissom, White, and Chaffee. These words are the price of admission to the ranks of Mission Control."

Ed Fendell, internal communications operator at Mission Control, remarked, "I think it [the tragedy] changed the entire attitude of who we were, and what we did, and how we progressed into the future of spaceflight."

And Chris Kraft remarked, "It's my opinion and an opinion of many others, had that not happened, we would never have gotten to the Moon. That interim period following the fire was the only thing that saved our ass, because we were able to then step back and say, 'What's wrong with this thing? What do we have to do to fix it?' And brought together the whole organization from top to bottom in NASA.

"Without all that happening, we'd never have gotten there [to the Moon]."[7]

One Giant Step for Mankind...

There were no manned flights for twenty months after the fire. Still, due to much of what they had learned from the tragedy of Apollo 1, NASA made a determined effort to make space flight safer.

Flights resumed in October 1968 with Apollo 7 testing the redesigned Command Module and Apollo 8 flying the Lunar Module in Moon orbit.

On July 20, 1969, astronauts Neil Armstrong and Buzz Aldrin flew Apollo 11 and walked on the Moon for the very first time in history.

"Houston, we've had a problem..."

As the Apollo program went forward, it progressed, though not without continued risks. But what happened in response to those risks changed significantly.

After Apollo 12 landed successfully on the Moon in November 1969, things had seemingly gotten back to "routine" at NASA. In the eyes of the American public, going into space to land on the Moon wasn't the extraordinary event it had been just a few months earlier.

Then, in April of 1970, just a little more than two days into its mission to land on the Moon, Apollo 13 had an unexpected catastrophe.

The Apollo mission was commanded by Jim Lovell with Command Module Pilot Jack Swigert and Lunar Module Pilot Fred Haise. The vehicle was made up of two independent spacecraft joined by a tunnel: The Odyssey (the command module sitting on top of the service module) was one unit and the other was the Eagle (LEM—Lunar Excursion Module).

During a routine procedure, the Service Module's number two oxygen tank exploded, crippling the Service Module that was providing life support to the crew. They notified Mission Control with the now famous words, "Houston, we've had a problem."

The astronauts were in mortal danger.

The result: the original mission to land on the Moon was aborted, and the new mission became to get the astronauts home *alive*.

The three astronauts abandoned the Command Module for the close confines of the Lunar Module to save energy and oxygen while NASA worked at Mission Control to figure out a plan. And due in part to the experience and what they had learned from the Apollo 1 tragedy, they came up with a way to get the astronauts back.

Flight director Gene Kranz (the flight director who was on the team when the Apollo 1 tragedy occurred) managed the highly intense and risk-laden process of getting the astronauts back.

Obviously, there were limited resources in space. They had to make do with what they had but use it *differently* and not in the way it was designed to be used. But NASA was able to quickly respond and come up with creative solutions, again, based on what they had learned from the Apollo 1 disaster.

After three agonizing days of NASA, vendors, and others working around the clock, Lovell, Haise, and Swigert returned safely to Earth on April 17.

According to Jim Lovell's book *Lost Moon*, as the Apollo 13's capsule landed in the ocean and the astronauts saw water running down the outside of their portholes, Lovell quietly pronounced the end of the mission: "Fellows, we're home."

But here's what caught my attention in this extraordinary story:

At the end of Ron Howard's excellent *Apollo 13* movie, Jim Lovell (played by Tom Hanks) steps off the rescue helicopter onto the deck of the USS Iwo Jima after being plucked out of the Pacific Ocean.

He narrates his final comments and says the Apollo 13 mission will become known as NASA's most *"successful failure."* He says:

"Our mission was called a *successful failure,* in that we returned safely but never made it to the Moon. In the following months, it was determined that a damaged coil built inside the oxygen tank sparked during our cryo stir and caused the explosion that crippled the Odyssey. It was a minor defect that occurred two years before I was even named the flight's commander...

"As for me, the seven extraordinary days of Apollo 13 were my last in space. I watched other men walk on the Moon, and return safely, all from the confines of Mission Control and our house in Houston. I sometimes catch myself looking up at the Moon, remembering the changes of fortune in our long voyage, thinking of the thousands of people who worked to bring the three of us home. I look up at the Moon and wonder, when will we be going back, and who will that be?"

***

Jeff Bezos *loves* space. Would he like to be one of those people going back?

The answer is yes, and it is undeniable that he applies the same "successful failure" principle to his business strategy.

Risk is not something to be taken lightly and Bezos doesn't take risk lightly.

As with NASA, there are truly life and death risks in many situations.

But the process of failure, and learning from failure, is when the *most profound learning takes place.*

From what he's written in the Shareholder Letters and elsewhere, Bezos believes in the concept of "successful failure." The learning process is so important he *intentionally* builds failure into his business model.

If he tries something and it works, that's great. But if he tries something and it doesn't work, he looks for ways not only to make it work but to make it *worth* it.

In a December 2014 interview with Henry Blodget, cofounder and publisher of *Business Insider*, Bezos talked about the role of failure in Amazon. He told Blodget,

> "...one of my jobs is to encourage people to be bold. It's incredibly hard. Experiments are, by their very nature, prone to failure. A few big successes compensate for dozens and dozens of things that didn't work.[8]"

In other words, he builds "experimenting" into his business model, knowing from the start that many of them will fail. Bezos also believes risk and failure are essential to business growth. In his words:

"What really matters is, companies that don't continue to experiment, companies that don't embrace failure, they eventually get in a desperate position where the only thing they can do is a Hail Mary bet at the very end of their corporate existence. Whereas companies that are making bets all along, even big bets, but not bet-the-company bets, prevail. I don't believe in bet-the-company bets. That's when you're desperate. That's the last thing you can do." —2014 *Business Insider* IGNITION conference

Too many companies only stay afloat when everything goes well. If something goes wrong, cashflow slows down, money gets tight, and sacrifices must be made. To the point where if some businesses even experience a "hiccup," they can be out of business almost just that fast.

Again, Amazon builds "failure" into its budgets to give it the flexibility to allocate resources to many things they know will fail. Not only will the few successes overcome the multiple failures, but Amazon learns from, and builds upon, its failures to make other endeavors successful.

Amazon's "R&D" department is essentially the whole company—every person who works for Amazon, including Jeff Bezos.

Amazon's Most Successful Failures

Amazon lost major money in two successive (but ultimately *successful)* failures.

The first of those two failures was Amazon's attempt to compete with eBay in 1999.

Dubbed *Amazon Auctions*, it was launched essentially to rival eBay's platform, albeit with several improvements. Amazon Auctions did attract many sellers and several buyers but, in the end, it just couldn't compete with eBay. Even Bezos remarked in the Blodget interview that Amazon Auctions "didn't work out very well."

While many factors contributed to its failure, one thing many agree on is that consumers were uncomfortable bidding on products using Amazon. When consumers shopped on Amazon, they expected to choose a product and pay a fixed price, and a low one. The desire for price certainty was important for Amazon customers.

People who shopped on eBay, on the other hand, had a different shopping mindset. They were willing to bid on items, especially unique ones, even if they ultimately lost the sale. Consumers were used to *bidding* on products using eBay and *buying* products using Amazon. They were not able to make the mindset shift to buying a different way on Amazon.

So, like that "root canal with no anesthesia," Amazon Auctions failed.

Amazon ditched the auction model and transitioned to another experiment called zShops, its second failure.

zShops was a creative attempt by Amazon to allow third-party sellers to use Amazon's large and growing platform. It was a huge risk for Amazon to allow other "sellers" to sell on Amazon's "store."

With zShops, third-party sellers could list their products using a unique landing page on Amazon's site with a separate log-in and search engine. They were separate from Amazon and paid a small fee to Amazon to use their platform.

Customers didn't like the additional steps required, and zShops was closed as a failure.

However, after shuttering zShops, the idea of allowing third parties to sell on Amazon would survive—and thrive into *billions* of dollars—as Amazon Marketplace.

A $178 Million Failure

Amazon's biggest failure from a monetary standpoint was the Fire Phone, which forced a $178 million write-off for the year, $170 million of which occurred in *one fiscal quarter.*

Amazon's Fire Phone, when released, was $649 in an exclusive arrangement with AT&T for only AT&T customers. It was called a "shopping machine" because it was really designed to help people shop on Amazon when they were out and about.

The phone was initially announced on stage by Jeff Bezos in June 2014. It had decent specifications for that time, such as having multiple cameras surrounding the phone display that created a sort of three-dimensional illusion. But this "dynamic perspective" feature seemed to be nothing more than a tech gimmick. Obviously, with a $178 million write-off, sales were very weak.

Amazon had tried to shore up sales and added a contract option in September 2014 where they lowered the contract price to $0.99. In October they dropped the non-contract price to $199.

The continued disappointing sales reflected a major problem: no one wanted it, and no one bought it.

In an October 2014 *Fortune* magazine article, Amazon Senior VP of Devices and Services, David Limp, acknowledged that Amazon bumbled the phone's pricing. According to the same article, Amazon's Fire Phone only got a two-star customer rating on Amazon's own site.

The Fire Phone was one of Amazon's big bets that ultimately failed. And it hurt.

In Amazon's 2014 10-K annual filing to the SEC they stated, "We recorded charges related to Fire Phone inventory valuation and supplier commitment costs, substantially all of which, $170 million, was recorded during the third quarter of 2014."

Amazon's official position on the Fire Phone is that the occasional face plant is part of the job (a.k.a. a "successful failure").

So, how exactly was it a "successful failure"?

Well, the team that created the Fire Phone took what they learned and eventually put it into the Echo hardware and Alexa to the tune of *billions* of dollars of revenue.

Successful Failure as a Mindset for Success

Just to be clear, failure isn't about incompetence or laziness. In fact, Amazon has an "intolerance for incompetence." In Amazon's case, failure is expected when new ideas or ways are tried. But Amazon will not tolerate anything less than giving your very best.

Given a 600,000-plus staff that's "competent" and an environment that's safe to try new things without fear, who knows?

Jeff Bezos, and Amazon, could be the first private company to land on the Moon.

APPLICATION

Encourage "Successful Failure"

Q: Do a "tolerance for failure" inventory at your company. How is failure handled?

Q: When is the last time you used a failure as a "case study" to improve your business?

Q: What can you do in your company or business to communicate that failure is an opportunity to learn and improve?

For more resources, go to TheBezosLetters.com

Chapter Two

Principle 2: Bet on Big Ideas

"After two decades of risk taking and teamwork, and with generous helpings of good fortune all along the way, we are now happily wed to what I believe are three such life partners: Marketplace, Prime, and AWS. Each of these offerings was a **bold bet** at first, and sensible people worried (often!) that they could not work. But at this point, it's become pretty clear how special they are and how lucky we are to have them."
—Bezos (2014 Letter)

Amazon Marketplace launched in November 2000 and has experienced a meteoric rise. After failing to launch third-party selling through zShops, what made Amazon Marketplace successful? ("Success" being defined as Marketplace going from 3 percent of sales in '99 to 58 percent of sales in 2018.)

The big difference was that third-party sellers' items appear *on the same page* as an Amazon item to people looking to buy something. There was one listing per item with Amazon Marketplace, unlike zShops, which created a new listing for each seller. That simple change made third-party transactions a much smoother experience all around. No longer would a customer need to go to a different part of the Amazon website to compare prices for the same product.

With Amazon Marketplace, customers had a choice: they could choose to purchase an item directly from Amazon or they could choose to order from a third-party seller. If a third-party seller had a lower price, or if Amazon was out of stock, Amazon would lose the sale. This allowed any seller to access Amazon's millions of daily customers.

But by astute design, Amazon earned a small commission from the third-party sellers who participated in the program (even if Amazon lost the sale). Third-party sellers were happy to pay the commission to use Amazon's platform, and Amazon was happy to collect it.

It worked. Today, Amazon Marketplace is home to thousands of individual sellers and large businesses alike selling products on Amazon.com.

But, not just anyone can sell in the Marketplace.

Every merchant needs to be prepared to meet Amazon's exacting standards.

Amazon is *obsessed* with customer experience. If you're going be a merchant in Amazon Marketplace, you need to be similarly obsessed because Amazon will protect its customers at all costs. Knowing this makes customers comfortable buying from third parties in the Marketplace and protects Amazon's hard-won positioning.

Not surprisingly, when the idea of third-party sellers was originally conceived, there were many within Amazon who thought it was a horrible idea. Why would Amazon give up very valuable screen "real estate" to competitors?

But here's the brilliance. Sellers on the Amazon Marketplace pay a fee to Amazon to access their customer base and fulfillment infrastructure. On average, sellers pay Amazon about 15 percent of *every item sold*. With more than half of the items sold on Amazon coming from third-party sellers, that percentage adds up.

Again, Marketplace started in 1999, and by the end of 2001 Amazon Marketplace orders grew to 6 percent of domestic orders, "far surpassing our expectations when we launched Amazon Marketplace," according to Bezos.

By 2018, *58 percent of units sold* on Amazon worldwide were from third-party sellers… creating billions of dollars in revenue for Amazon.

Amazon Auctions and zShops were undeniably "successful failures" that paid off.

Betting on Free Delivery: Super Saver Shipping and Amazon Prime

In 2002, Amazon had a wild idea it believed could forever change the way people shopped.

Eight years after founding Amazon in his garage, Bezos undoubtedly realized one of the biggest obstacles keeping people from shopping online was the cost of shipping.

Online shopping offered many conveniences to customers. It also helped businesses reduce overhead by being able to operate out of warehouses in rural areas where real estate and operations costs were relatively low. The customers needed to get the products they purchased, but shipping was expensive, and paying for shipping was also a psychological barrier.

The cost of shipping was one of the last big objections customers had to doing business with Amazon. Amazon got past the inability of customers to "touch and feel" products by using images and having liberal return policies. And the ease of shopping on Amazon was more convenient than having to drive to a physical store.

But, still, the cost of shipping was a turnoff to many customers and caused many people to continue to shop, and buy, at malls and local department stores. Even small shipping costs stopped many people from shopping online.

Bezos and his team had an idea to overcome this objection by offering free shipping on any order over $25—a big gamble for Amazon. Shipping wasn't cheap. It was also not a cost Amazon could control, either. Amazon needed to pay companies like FedEx, UPS, and the United States Postal Service to deliver products to customers. If those companies raised their rates, Amazon's costs could skyrocket.

Amazon introduced Super Saver Shipping (which was the slowest shipping method available) and required a minimum order of over $25 to help limit the risk of their big bet. However, this investment in free shipping was still a huge gamble.

The public responded—and in a very positive way. Amazon's customers started filling up their carts with products to cross the $25 threshold, which typically required someone to buy more than one item.

Three years later, free shipping had become so popular that Amazon doubled down on its big bet by launching *Amazon Prime*.

The question was: Would people pay (up front) to get "free shipping"?

For $79 per year, customers could subscribe to Amazon Prime and receive unlimited free two-day shipping and upgrade to one-day delivery for $3.99 per order.

Amazon's big bet on Amazon Prime paid off… in spades.

By the end of 2018, Amazon boasted more than 100 million Amazon Prime members. It also raised the price of an Amazon Prime subscription to $119 per year, or $12.99 per month. What's remarkable is that Amazon Prime members spent an average of $1,400 per year on Amazon in 2018 compared to only $600 per year for non-Prime customers.

When Bezos bet big on free shipping, he believed it would help Amazon overcome one of the biggest customer hurdles, the cost of shipping. And when he offered two-day shipping through Amazon Prime, he believed he could make free shipping even more convenient for customers. The foray into Amazon Prime was quite risky at first and it wasn't always "sunshine and roses."

And here's a startling fact: In 2018 alone, Amazon spent $27.7 *billion* in shipping costs.

But Amazon Prime is now a foundational Amazon offering, expanding to include thirty-five additional benefits, including video streaming, and generating billions of dollars in revenue from subscription fees and the revenue from Amazon Prime members.

In his 2014 Letter, Bezos reflected on Amazon Prime and their free-shipping bets:

"Ten years ago, we launched Amazon Prime, originally designed as an all-you-can-eat free and fast shipping program. We were told repeatedly that it was a risky move, and in some ways it was. In its first year, we gave up many millions of dollars in shipping revenue, and there was no simple math to show that it would be worth it.

"Our decision to go ahead was built on the positive results we'd seen earlier when we introduced Free Super Saver Shipping, and an intuition that customers would quickly grasp that they were being offered the best deal in the history of shopping. In addition, analysis told us that, if we achieved scale, we would be able to significantly lower the cost of fast shipping." —Bezos (2014 Letter)

Redefining shipping for the customer was a big bet, but one that eventually paid off in spades.

Betting on Leveraging Infrastructure: Amazon Web Services

"...all AWS services are pay-as-you-go and radically transform capital expense into a variable cost. AWS is self-service: you don't need to negotiate a contract or engage with the salesperson—you can just read the online documentation to get started. AWS services are elastic—they easily scale up and easily scale down." —Bezos (2011 Letter)

Free shipping wasn't the only big idea Amazon bet on throughout the years. Bezos and his team continued to believe they could change the world and grow Amazon to new heights.

Bezos has always had criteria and tests that have to be passed for Amazon to enter a new business market. In 2014, he said (bullets are mine):

"A dreamy business offering has at least four characteristics.
- Customers love it,
- it can grow to very large size,
- it has strong returns on capital,
- and it's durable in time—with the potential to endure for decades."
—Bezos (2014 Letter)

Technology has always been the heartbeat of Amazon. Obviously, with an online business, it's all about the tech. But in the early years, tech (IT) was an expense, not a profit center.

Internally at Amazon, the gatekeepers in the IT department were a bottleneck that prevented other departments from growing as rapidly as they needed. Like most companies at the time, the IT group controlled computing resources, but with the rapid growth of Amazon, that bottleneck was becoming a huge problem that exasperated employees, including Jeff Bezos.

In Brad Stone's informative book *The Everything Store,* he talks about how around that time Bezos came across a book called *Creation,* by Steve Grand (it wasn't about the biblical book of Genesis, it was about a video game called *Creatures*). The book appeared to be what triggered Bezos' and Amazon's approach to cloud computing by suggesting setting up an infrastructure that reduced the tech to bite-size pieces (no pun intended) so developers could use them as foundation building blocks with the flexibility necessary for "do it yourself" services.

The process of creating a centralized development platform that can be used by any group within the company was started. Internal teams at Amazon needed common infrastructure services that everyone could access without reinventing the wheel. Every department was different but needed the same kind of tech services. That is precisely what Amazon set out to build. And that's when they began to realize they may have something more significant.

At an executive retreat in 2003, Amazon's executive team went through an exercise to identify the company's core competencies. They knew they could offer a broad selection of products. They were good at fulfilling and shipping orders, but as they dug into the organization, they realized they had also become very skilled at running a reliable, scalable, cost-efficient data center. Because Amazon is such a low margin business, the datacenters and services they created had to be as lean and efficient as possible.

Amazon Web Services was created to provide on-demand cloud computing to individuals, companies, and governments on a metered pay-as-you-go basis… and a new business was born.

"With AWS, we're building a new business focused on a new customer set...software developers. We're targeting broad needs universally faced by developers, such as storage and compute capacity—areas in which developers have asked for help, and in which we have deep expertise from scaling Amazon.com over the last twelve years. We're well-positioned to do it, it's highly differentiated, and it can be a significant, financially attractive business over time." —Bezos (2006 Letter)

How does that translate for consumers? Bezos said,

"A radical idea when it was launched nine years ago, Amazon Web Services is now big and growing fast. Startups were the early adopters. On-demand, pay-as-you-go cloud storage and compute resources dramatically increased the speed of starting a new business. Companies like Pinterest, Dropbox, and Airbnb all used AWS services and remain customers today." —Bezos (2014 Letter)

Did his big bet on AWS pay off? Bezos said,

"I believe AWS is one of those dreamy business offerings that can be serving customers and earning financial returns for many years into the future. Why am I optimistic? For one thing, the size of the opportunity is big, ultimately encompassing global spend on servers, networking, datacenters, infrastructure software, databases, data warehouses, and more. Similar to the way I think about Amazon retail, for all practical purposes, I believe AWS is market-size unconstrained." —Bezos (2014 Letter)

Bet Little on Big Ideas

The biggest takeaway from how Amazon bets on big ideas is that, even when an idea has great potential, Bezos starts his bets small, at least in relative terms.

With free shipping, Amazon started by experimenting with free Super Saver Shipping on orders over $25. When they experienced success with that, they bet bigger with Amazon Prime. The more that idea paid off, the more Amazon invested into it, adding streaming videos and other services and raising subscription prices over time.

Amazon's made *billions* of dollars off Amazon Marketplace, Amazon Prime, and Amazon Web Services. Amazon Auctions lost a lot of money in real terms but nothing Amazon couldn't bounce back from.

Like Bezos said about failure, "None of those things are fun. But they also don't matter."

The Next Big Bets

In the 1979 hit song *The Gambler,* Kenny Rogers famously said, "You've got to know when to hold 'em; Know when to fold 'em; Know when to walk away; And know when to run."

Bezos does this by setting criteria through which he evaluates big bets. And there's no better example of this than how Bezos has handled an issue many people had asked him about for years—expanding into physical stores.

Before talking specifically about physical stores, Bezos summarized Amazon's approach to business:

"At Amazon's current scale, planting seeds that will grow into meaningful new businesses takes some discipline, a bit of patience, and a nurturing culture.

"Our established businesses are well-rooted young trees. They are growing, enjoy high returns on capital, and operate in very large market segments. These characteristics set a high bar for any new business we would start. Before we invest our shareholders' money in a new business, we must convince ourselves that the new opportunity can generate the returns on capital our investors expected when they invested in Amazon. And we must convince ourselves that the new business can grow to a scale where it can be significant in the context of our overall company.

"Furthermore, we must believe that the opportunity is currently underserved and that we have the capabilities needed to bring strong customer-facing differentiation to the marketplace. Without that, it's unlikely we'd get to scale in that new business." —Bezos (2006 Letter)

From there, Bezos immediately shifted to the topic of physical stores, saying:

"I often get asked, 'When are you going to open physical stores?' That's an expansion opportunity we resisted. It fails all but one of the tests...

"The potential size of a network of physical stores is exciting. However, we don't know how to do it with low capital and high returns; physical world retailing is a cagey and ancient business that's already well served; and we don't have any ideas for how to build a physical-world store experience that's meaningfully differentiated for customers." —Bezos (2006 Letter)

What this suggests is that, while many believed Amazon was not interested in opening physical stores, the reality is Bezos had yet to find a way to do so that was consistent with the criteria through which he evaluated any new business. Thus, he used discipline and patience to resist taking an unwise risk, instead waiting until the moment was right to take a smart risk.

Fast forward, and Amazon has moved to create a number of physical store locations, starting with Amazon physical bookstores, Amazon Go Stores, and now including (by acquisition) purchasing Whole Foods, a perfect example of waiting for an opportunity that fit Amazon's criteria for taking a smaller risk at first and *then* scaling and betting big—$13.4 billion big.

Searching for the Fourth Big Bet

"Marketplace, Prime, and Amazon Web Services are three big ideas. We're lucky to have them, and we're determined to improve and nurture them—make them even better for customers. You can also count on us to **work hard to find a fourth**. We've already got a number of candidates in work, and as we promised some twenty years ago, we'll continue to make bold bets." —Bezos (2014 Letter)

APPLICATION

Bet on Big Ideas

Q. When is the last time you bet on a really big idea?

Q: What can you do to encourage your team (or even yourself) to be willing to explore new big ideas?

Q: What is a big idea right now that you'd be willing to bet on?

For more resources, go to TheBezosLetters.com

Chapter Three

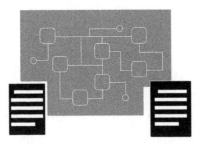

Principle 3: Practice Dynamic Invention and Innovation

"One area where I think we are especially distinctive is failure. I believe we are the best place in the world to fail (we have plenty of practice!), and **failure and invention are inseparable twins**. To invent you have to experiment, and if you know in advance that it's going to work, it's not an experiment." —Bezos (2015 Letter)

When many people think of Thomas Edison, they think of the inventor of the light bulb. While it's true he gets credit for inventing the light bulb, he was actually the person responsible for creating the filaments that made the light bulb economically viable to the mainstream market.

Edison was a prolific inventor. He's often quoted as having said, "If I find 10,000 ways something won't work, I haven't failed. I am not discouraged, because every wrong attempt discarded is often a step forward."

He wasn't kidding about the "10,000 ways that won't work." That's why he's known as the "Wizard of Menlo Park," his personal idea factory, for the rate in which he collected patents and accumulated credit for inventions. He was awarded 1,039 patents in his eighty-four years. And while he deserves much of the credit, the way he reached such a prolific rate is perhaps one of lesser known stories in U.S. history.

While the vision most people have of Edison is a wise sage in the late 1800s and early 1900s sitting alone in a laboratory questioning how things worked, actually the real story is much different.

Edison was brilliant and smart enough to not try and do everything he wanted to do alone. Far from the vision of an old genius sitting in a solitary room, Edison built a series of laboratories in West Orange, New Jersey, in 1887. He then staffed those laboratories starting out with thirty-five people, and he ended up employing thousands of people over the years in what has been described as an "invention factory."

It was at that point that his experimentation reached a systematic, industrial scale. Every storeroom was well stocked (remarkable for the time) so his team of experimenters had everything they needed to test and explore.

Thus, Edison may more accurately be described as the father of commercial research and as the world's most prolific inventor. He also commented more directly on the industrialization of the trial-and-error process, saying, "The real measure of success is the number of experiments that can be crowded into twenty-four hours."

Roughly two hundred years later, Jeff Bezos has taken the same type of commercial approach to invention and innovation.

Rather than creating one department of people tasked with innovating the company's offerings and operations (a typical corporate Research & Development department), Bezos encourages experimentation at *all* levels of the organization and in *all* departments—basically anyone who gets a paycheck from Amazon. He makes invention a part of each person's job description, and it's a core principle that helped Amazon grow.

So, what's the difference between invention and innovation?

- They're linked together, but it seems that invention can be defined as something new, the creation of a product or introduction of a process for the first time.
- Innovation is when someone improves upon or makes a significant contribution to an existing product, service, or process.
- And both of these, invention and innovation, need a culture, environment, and mindset to make it all possible.

In 2011, when talking specifically about the Kindle, Bezos gives us a clue on his thoughts when he says:

"Amazonians are leaning into the future, with radical and transformational innovations that create value for thousands of authors, entrepreneurs, and developers. Invention has become second nature at Amazon, and in my view the team's pace of innovation is even accelerating—I can assure you it's very energizing." —Bezos (2011)

A core value for Amazon is that dynamic invention and innovation means everyone is looking for improvement, all the time.

At Amazon, invention (and innovation) are ingrained into the daily culture from the first day on the job. It doesn't matter if you are a recent college graduate newly hired or a seasoned sales representative. Bezos expects you to look at every task and ask how you can make it better or more efficient.

What can you experiment with that will get you better results? Amazon wants the kind of person who will ask that question. In fact, questioning the status quo is practically required. Everyone is encouraged to try new things, ask questions, and look at processes differently from the get-go.

And if you try something and it doesn't work? Don't worry. If your attitude is good and you're sincerely trying, your failure is more likely to be celebrated than admonished. And it might turn out to be one of the successful failures Bezos has turned into billions of dollars in profits.

And if you try something new and it *does* work, Amazon expects you to share it with others to help the organization grow. You are encouraged to collect relevant data to support your conclusions, share it with your immediate supervisors, and test whether it is repeatable and reliable within a small group of peers.

If your initial data is confirmed at a smaller scale, you could be tasked with creating an entire training program for all employees.

Dynamic Invention Helps Unleash Creativity

Amazon's emphasis on practicing dynamic invention throughout the organization has been one of its foundational growth principles for many reasons, although two reasons stand out.

First, it helps identify your most inventive team members.

With more than 600,000 employees, it is much easier to encourage each of them to test and share their best ideas than to try to identify which of those 600,000-plus employees are the "inventors" coming up with new products, ideas, platforms or processes. Let the inventors rise up by encouraging everyone to suggest ways to create and improve (you may be surprised).

Second, it empowers the people who actually perform each task to come up with new ways to do their jobs or improve upon processes.

If you look closely, you will see the most productive workers doing *something* that helps them create newer, better, or faster ways to do their job than the others. No manager, without having been on the floor themselves, would be able to come up with new ideas by sitting in a conference room three floors up.

Of course, a trained eye usually can recognize the most productive employee and what makes them so productive. But the very best ideas are almost always initiated by people performing the tasks, rather than people in formal leadership positions. Amazon empowers its people to experiment and encourages them to share their best ideas so the entire organization can benefit.

Bezos is always looking for creative thinking. When he first started Amazon, he said,

> "I was packing boxes, on my hands and knees with somebody else in our next segment kneeling next to me. We're packing and I said, 'You know, we need knee pads. This is killing my knees.' And this guy packing alongside me said, 'We need packing tables.' And I was like, that's the most brilliant idea I've ever heard!" —2018 Interview, *The David Rubenstein Show*, Bloomberg[9]

Be Intentional about Dynamic Invention

Virtually every company knows they need to be inventive and innovative to survive. Knowledge is not the issue that keeps companies from inventing like Amazon. Desire is not the issue that keeps companies from inventing like Amazon. What keeps companies from inventing like Amazon is creating the corporate culture and structure that allows invention and innovation to flourish at all levels of the organization.

Amazon takes extraordinary steps to develop an internal culture that promotes innovative thinking, freedom to experiment, and freedom to fail. It is imperative that the true culture of an organization allows for testing out new ideas even if they seem "crazy." It is critical that the experimentation be done without fear of someone's career being derailed if they don't get something right the first time.

To practice dynamic invention in your organization, you must both empower your team to experiment and make sure *failure is not fatal.*

Here's what my friend and business associate Kurt Huffman said:

"People are afraid of the *consequences* of failure. People are afraid of being fired, ridiculed, hurt, black-listed, demoted, etc. People may still not like failure. I don't 'like' failure. But when I know the consequences of my failure are seen as learning opportunities rather than a pink slip, it facilitates rather than stifles innovation."

If employees (including management) experiment and fail, they are encouraged to share their thinking and results with their team leader, team members, or peers. That collective wisdom of people closest to the task they attempted to improve can help identify what went wrong. Or they can help identify how to turn the failure into a "successful failure" that provides other benefits to the organization.

It is critical that everyone both "talk the talk and walk the walk." If you admonish or discipline an employee or a peer for experimenting in good faith, that will be the last time they attempt to innovate or try something new and creative. If others get wind that the reaction to failure was criticism or punishment, they will quickly stop looking for ways to improve as well.

Instead, encourage people to take smart risks because the reality is the biggest risk most businesses make today is not taking *enough* risk.

Leverage Your Advantages

Again, Amazon is currently experimenting, inventing, and innovating with retail physical bookstore locations. The company that was initially known for online book sales is now opening up retail stores. What are they seeing in the marketplace now that is prompting them to experiment with physical bookstores?

For one thing, people don't go into an Amazon bookstore if they know what they want to read; they just order on Amazon. They visit Amazon Books, the physical bookstore, to find out what they want to read *next*.

I have personally visited several Amazon (physical) bookstores in Chicago, New York City, and Washington, DC, and here are a few things that make Amazon Books different from the traditional "brick and mortar" bookstore:

- All the books are "facing out" so you can see the cover, not just the spine with the title of the book. This means they can't stock as many books. But, in testing, they found that consumers liked being able to see the book covers.
- Stores are smaller than say a Barnes & Noble because they don't have to stock multiples of books; any book can be ordered by a customer using terminals in the store.
- Amazon Books only stocks highly rated books in the store— only a 4.6 or higher out of a 5-star rating on Amazon. Nothing less makes it onto the shelves. It could even be a *New York Times* best-selling book, but if it doesn't make 4.6 or higher on Amazon's site, it doesn't make it into their bookstore.
- Every book has a placard with a QR code that displays data about the book including all the reviews that you can access from your phone or tablet. You can "read more about it" while looking at the actual book.

- Amazon already knows what people in the geographic area are reading, so the store stocks locally popular titles. Each store is able to tailor the selection on the shelves based on local interests.
- In addition to books, Amazon Books also sells their hardware items such as Fire TV, Echoes, etc., and other popular electronic gadgets.

Amazon is doing what inventive companies do—they experiment and test to see what works best for their customers and what might improve the customer experience.

Why Practicing Dynamic Invention and Innovation is Essential

Invention and innovation come in many different ways and iterations. When Bezos talks about the "The Power of Invention" he says,

"Invention comes in many forms and at many scales. The most radical and transformative of inventions are often those that empower others to unleash their creativity—to pursue their dreams. That's a big part of what's going on with Amazon Web Services, Fulfillment by Amazon, and Kindle Direct Publishing. With AWS, FBA, and KDP, we are creating powerful self-service platforms that allow thousands of people to boldly experiment and accomplish things that would otherwise be impossible or impractical. These innovative, large-scale platforms are not zero-sum—they create win-win situations and create significant value for developers, entrepreneurs, customers, authors, and readers." —Bezos (2011 Letter)

Practicing dynamic invention is evident at every level at Amazon. Creating something new and improving upon what you're currently doing is at the very core of what it takes to grow like Amazon.

Lessons learned from previous failures help mitigate losses and improve plans for future experiments, making the next projects more likely to succeed.

Amazon knows that invention and innovation require experimentation, experimentation requires failure, and learning requires tracking and measuring your results.

Lab126—Amazon's Invention Lab

Competitive advantage is paramount to companies like Amazon, Apple, Google, etc. And that doesn't happen when everyone knows what you're working on. ("Skunkworks" is the nickname for places where there's always something "secret" being worked on.)

In 2004, Amazon wanted to "improve upon the physical book, making it easier than ever for customers to discover and enjoy books"… and thus began Lab126, their secretive San Francisco Bay Area research and development center for *hardware and consumer electronic devices,* the first of which was the Kindle.[10]

This was a leap for Amazon as they experimented with creating a product for the physical world and not being solely focused on the online world.

Insiders called their first experiment "Project A," which was the Kindle (in 2007), "Project B" was the Fire Phone (a.k.a. "successful failure"), and "Project D" was the Echo, to name a few. (There's speculation about a "Project C" but nothing has come of it… yet.)[11]

The Lab126 name came from the "swoosh" arrow in the Amazon logo, which draws a happy-looking line from A to Z in "Amazon." In Lab126, the "1" stands for "A" and the "26" stands for "Z."

Lab126 is always on the cutting edge of invention and innovation. In fact, they may be working on a "Project X, or Y, or Z" right now with hopes that it will be the next wave of delivering on the promise to always serve the customer and create new and exciting products and services on their behalf.

I think if Thomas Edison and Jeff Bezos were to have ever met, they would have found they had a thing or two in common.

APPLICATION

Practice Dynamic Invention and Innovation

Q: Set aside time in the next thirty days to ask yourself: What is the next new thing I want to try in my business?

Q: How can you set up a "Lab126" in your company?

For more resources, go to TheBezosLetters.com

Growth Cycle: Build

Obsess Over Customers

Apply Long-Term Thinking

Understand Your Flywheel

At Amazon, building is how you turn promising ideas into stable initiatives. Amazon builds by making sure everything they invest in is based on what its customers actually *want*.

The great news is that short-term risks help discover which initiatives are likely to be winners so the losers can be eliminated (and learned from)—a savings of time, energy, and capital in the bigger picture.

Amazon uses long-term thinking to ensure each initiative (and risk) is built on a solid foundation that can be around for years and beyond, even if that means sacrificing in the short-term.

Bezos is not interested in building anything that will *only* make money in the short-term. In fact, Amazon makes sure each initiative is consistent with Amazon's core business model, which Bezos calls its "flywheel," a term coined by author Jim Collins in his book *Good to Great*. This approach to building makes Amazon an extremely focused and stable (yet nimble) company.

Chapter Four

Principle 4:
Obsess Over Customers

"I constantly remind our employees to be afraid, to wake up every morning terrified. Not of our competition, but of our customers. **Our customers have made our business what it is,** they are the ones with whom we have a relationship, and they are the ones to whom we owe a great obligation. And we consider them to be loyal to us—right up until the second that someone else offers them a better service." —Bezos (1998 Letter)

"Working backwards from customer needs often demands that we acquire new competencies and exercise new muscles, never mind how uncomfortable and awkward-feeling those first steps might be." —Bezos (2008 Letter)

Amazon wants happy customers.

The iconic Amazon "swoosh" conveys through the smile and arrow that they are "delivering smiles to customers' doorsteps." When their updated logo was released in 2000, Amazon stated "a smile now begins under the a and ends with a dimple under the z, emphasizing that Amazon.com offers anything, from A to Z, that customers may be looking to buy online."[12]

In fact, happy customers are the pinnacle of what Amazon aspires to and Bezos wants everyone to be "*obsessed* with customers."

"Obsessive" is a clinical description of a focus that is way beyond "normal." The word "obsessive" often has a negative connotation in our vocabulary today. It means going overboard to the point of extremism.

But this is exactly how much Bezos wants everyone at Amazon to care about their customers and their needs.

Of all the Amazon Leadership Principles, perhaps the most important one has to do with Customer Obsession. The first job of a leader at Amazon is to be obsessed with their customers—and *everyone* at Amazon is expected to be a leader no matter what their role or job.

> *"Amazon Leadership Principle—*Customer Obsession: Leaders start with the customer and work backwards. They work vigorously to earn and keep customer trust. Although leaders pay attention to competitors, they obsess over customers."

Amazon's Leadership Principle of Customer Obsession works hand-in-hand with the Anderson Growth Principle of Obsess *Over* Customers because you can't grow **any** business without customers.

Being a Customer-Obsessed Business

The real secret to Amazon's customer obsession is not in the conceptual but the practical execution.

"Obsession," in the truest sense, describes Amazon's focus on being persistent and preoccupied with the wants and needs of customers—often even before the customers themselves know what it is they want.

Everything Amazon does in both the big and small picture can be traced back to something Amazon either knows or believes about its customers.

Becoming a customer-obsessed business requires you to get into your customers' heads. Consider asking questions about what your customer really wants in order to become customer-obsessed. For some questions, you might be able to immediately provide an answer you think is what the customer would say. But you won't know until you get it straight from the horse's mouth (or the horse's *data*).

Most companies in business today say they care about their customers. Look no further than the cliché many businesses espouse, "The customer is always right." But lip service to a cliché phrase is much different from a *proactive* obsession with customers. "The customer is always right" is reactive. It tells employees to defer to customers who approach the business with a concern.

I was recently at a recruiting event in Nashville and heard Dave Johnson, an Amazon executive, say that before he came to Amazon, he had worked for two big-name companies that were customer-focused and they were *really* good. "But," he said, "at Amazon… we are customer-*obsessed*."

Emphasizing customer obsession allows Amazon employees to become *solution-focused rather than problem-focused*. Bezos wants to always be ahead of the game… he wants to "solve problems before they happen," meaning he doesn't want screw-ups to happen in the first place.

But wanting happy customers and actually delivering on that premise can be tricky.

Amazon created the Customer Experience Pillars in order to focus on exactly what their customers want and deliver it to them.

In 2001, Amazon was clear that they were building on two pillars of customer experience: selection and convenience. But Bezos then added one more pillar: relentlessly lowering prices.

The three Customer Experience Pillars are:

- Low Prices
- Best Selection
- Fast Convenient Delivery

"In our retail business, we have strong conviction that customers value low prices, vast selection, and fast, convenient delivery and that these needs will remain stable over time. It is difficult for us to imagine that ten years from now, customers will want higher prices, less selection, or slower delivery. Our belief in the durability of these pillars is what gives us the confidence required to invest in strengthening them. We know that the energy we put in now will continue to pay dividends well into the future." —Bezos (2008 Letter)

What Do Customers *Really* Want?

Too many companies mistakenly focus on their products and services over their customers. When designing or improving products, they make existing *features* better. Then they spend time and money marketing new features. When customers don't buy, executives from those companies may think the problem is their messaging. Or they may think customers don't understand how valuable their product or service is.

Many times, the problem is not the messaging or their customers' lack of understanding; the problem is the company considered, as an afterthought, what the customer wanted or needed. That kind of company is not customer-obsessed; it is product-obsessed.

Here are the questions Amazon *always* asks:

- Who is the customer?
- What is the customer problem or opportunity?
- What is the most important customer benefit? (singular)
- How do you know what the customer needs?
- What does the customer experience look like?

Customer Service as an Extension of Customer Obsession

What do your customers want from their first contact with customer service? Chances are, one of their most important desires is to get their problem solved quickly, with as little hassle as possible, and in a way that is best for *them* (chat, email, phone, etc.).

For example, Amazon knows most people hate being "on hold." Even if it's a short wait, you don't want to have to "sit on hold" waiting for someone to take your call. The way Amazon works, if you place a phone call to Amazon customer service, you don't have to wait on the line. You put in your phone number and Amazon calls *you* back almost immediately.

But here's what's important to understand: Amazon sees a customer needing to call them with a problem as a *failure in their system.*

Amazon wants the customer to be able to solve the problem on their own, or have Amazon automatically realize there is a problem, proactively solve it, and have their issue resolved without needing to be transferred several times.

That said, some customers might want to talk to an actual human to feel they are truly being heard (whether by chat, email, or by phone). Amazon offers multiple options for customer service.

Amazon knows if customers have to work too hard to find a way to contact you to resolve their problem quickly, they will be dissatisfied, and their frustration can go viral faster than lightning.

However, if customers have issues resolved by customer service, you will see lower return rates, more positive mentions of your company on social media (even when there were problems), better online reviews, and more repeat customers. That's what Amazon is counting on.

But more than that, Bezos knows the key to growth and success is not having more customer service representatives to solve problems, but to eliminate those problems before they become widespread.

For example, during customer service calls or online chats, instead of blindly following checklists or scripts, representatives are empowered to do whatever they can to best serve the customer.

My wife (who hates going shopping but loves to shop online on Amazon) just recently had an experience where she ordered decaffeinated coffee and got regular. She did a customer service chat and the coffee was replaced, and the representative added that if she got the wrong product again to please contact them and they would pull it from the system and investigate the problem.

When she, in fact, got the wrong coffee again, she called them on the phone and spoke with an Amazon representative who pulled it from the system, replaced it with a different brand, and gave her a credit for the difficulty she experienced with her order.

Yes, it was inconvenient for her but she came away happy because she felt they not only listened to her, they were responsive to what the *bigger* problem was—and she felt they were actually going to fix the problem, not just make her happy and ignore the root cause. (As a bonus, she got to keep the caffeinated coffee to use for friends who wanted "high test.")

The result: she will keep ordering on Amazon with confidence (and she buys a *lot* on Amazon).

When a customer feels understood and respected, they are more likely to return to buy *more*. Part of Amazon's culture is that agents are authorized to solve many issues without needing to check with supervisors or get approval.

In the same way, Amazon expects their third-party merchants to be similarly obsessed. In fact, they *incentivize* third-party merchants who sell on Amazon's platform to care for their customers in the same way as they do.

For example, Amazon sent a letter to thousands of third-party merchants letting them know that as of August 1, 2019, select products sold and fulfilled by Amazon must comply with Frustration-Free Packaging. Remarkably, Amazon put its "money where its mouth is" providing vendors with an incentive credit to assist with transition costs if they comply by the August 1, 2019, deadline. Vendors who don't comply will experience an ongoing charge for each package that doesn't comply. Thus, Amazon is using Frustration-Free Packaging incentives to shift the competitive landscape for third-party vendors.

In some cases, Amazon actually *requires* third-party merchants to adopt customer-centric policies or risk being kicked off its platform. Amazon is quick to suspend or delist a merchant whose customer reviews turn negative and stay unresolved.

For Marketplace third-party merchants, it is critical for them to understand the Amazon customer-obsession *mindset* to be successful.

Keep Asking Questions

The other tenet Amazon incorporates into everything they do is to ask the question: What keeps customers from doing business with us?

The most obvious example early on was the objection to paying for shipping. That objection kept customers from doing business with them. The same was true for being able to "touch and feel" products before they bought them—customers weren't used to that.

So, what did Bezos and Amazon do? They did a number of things.

Again, they gave customers multiple ways to avoid paying for shipping and made shopping online less "painful."

They also first focused on books (products that were less "touch" sensitive) and offered previews, listing details, editorial reviews, and customer reviews to encourage people to help buy the right book for them. They also made returns simple and easy to help overcome the objection of hassling with a return.

This transfers the risk of dissatisfaction from the customer to Amazon. It takes advantage of Amazon's biggest value propositions, their three Customer Experience Pillars: low prices, best selection, and fast convenient delivery.

The Power of Automated Systems

> "We build automated systems that look for occasions when we've provided a customer experience that isn't up to our standards, and those systems then proactively refund customers." —Bezos (2012 Letter)

In December 2012, Henry Blodget wrote an article for BusinessInsider.com describing his experience with Amazon's proactive, automated systems.

Blodget had rented the movie *Casablanca* because he was writing a story about some simple business lessons from the movie that could save the American economy. He never intended to watch the movie straight through but started, stopped, rewound it, and fast forwarded through the movie to capture his points. And, like many streaming video players at the time, it often seized up, forcing him to rewind and start watching again.

While annoying, it was not unexpected; in 2012 the process of streaming video was clunky at best. It could have been a problem with the player, his internet connection speed, or something on Amazon's end.

"So, imagine my surprise this morning when I got the email below from Amazon.

—

Hello,

We noticed that you experienced poor video playback while watching the following rental(s) on Amazon video on demand: *Casablanca*
We're sorry for the inconvenience and have issued you a refund for the following amount(s): $2.99 … We hope to see you again soon."
Amazon Video on Demand Team

—

"Amazon 'noticed that I experienced poor video playback…' They did? And they decided to give a refund because of that? Wow."

Blodget explained what transpired in an article titled *Just the Latest Example of Why Amazon Is One of the Most Successful Companies in the World*. "Amazon is obsessed with making its customers happy. Unlike many other companies, Amazon will instantly trade off short-term profits for the chance to engender long-term customer loyalty."[13]

This story illustrates a convergence of several growth principles including customer obsession, long-term thinking, and high standards. All of these principles played a role in the impetus to create an automated system that monitors the quality of the customer interaction and responds automatically.

Beyond the Expected

This last sentence from Bezos' 2012 Letter caught my attention: "The drive to get the customer to say 'Wow'—keeps the pace of innovation fast."

It's not just serving the customer. Obsession is about always going beyond the norm—it's the kind of extremism that make Bezos happy. It's inventing on the customer's behalf, it's improving the customer experience, and it's getting the customer to say "Wow" because they've gotten more than they expected. And that's what I mean by "obsess *over* customers."

"We also have authors as customers. Amazon Publishing has just announced it will start paying authors their royalties monthly, sixty days in arrears. The industry standard is twice a year, and that has been the standard for a long time. Yet when we interview authors as customers, infrequent payment is a major dissatisfier. Imagine how you'd like it if you were paid twice a year. There isn't competitive pressure to pay authors more than once every six months, but we're proactively doing so.

"We've reduced AWS prices 27 times since launching 7 years ago, added enterprise service support enhancements, and created innovative tools to help customers be more efficient. AWS Trusted Advisor monitors customer configurations, compares them to known best practices, and then notifies customers where opportunities exist to improve performance, enhance security, or save money. Yes, we are actively telling customers they're paying us more than they need to. In the last 90 days, customers have saved millions of dollars through Trusted Advisor, and the service is only getting started.

"All of this progress comes in the context of AWS being the widely recognized leader in its area—a situation where you might worry that external motivation could fail. On the other hand, internal motivation—the drive to get the customer to say 'Wow'—keeps the pace of innovation fast." —Bezos (2012 Letter)

APPLICATION

Obsess Over Customers

Q: Sit down right now and write a description of your prototypical (good) customer. What are their three to four key traits? What are their biggest problems that you can help solve?

Q: What can you do today to improve that customer's experience with you?

Q: Challenge your team to come up with a new idea every week to super-serve your customers, no matter what the cost.

For more resources, go to TheBezosLetters.com

Chapter Five

Principle 5:
Apply Long-Term Thinking

"We believe that a fundamental measure of our success will be the shareholder value we create over the ***long term***." —Bezos (1997 Letter)

"We are working to build something important, something that matters to our customers, something that we can **all tell our grandchildren** about." —Bezos (1997 Letter)

By 1989, the turn of the century was only eleven years away, and inventor and computer scientist Danny Hillis had already grown frustrated by the way people talked about the year 2000. His whole childhood, he heard person after person use the year 2000 as the singular measure of the future. For thirty years, he recalled people talking about the actual year 2000, but nobody was mentioning anything *beyond* the year 2000.[14]

At the time, although many people likely didn't pay much attention to the year 2000 references, Hillis did. In his words, "everybody talked about what would happen by the year 2000 but no one mentions a future date at all. The future has been shrinking by one year per year for my entire life."

While most of the world focused on the year 2000 itself and what might happen if computers failed when the date turned over from 1999 to 2000 (dubbed Y2K), the fact is, once the world became aware of the potential problem, computers were simply (or, in many cases, not-so-simply) reprogrammed to avoid the issue.

But Hillis felt compelled to get people thinking *past* the year 2000, which he described as a "mental barrier of an ever-shortening future."

So, he built what has become known as the **10,000 Year Clock**.

The *10,000 Year Clock* is a clock "powered by mechanical energy harvested from sunlight as well as the people that visit it."[15] As the name suggests, the clock is designed to run for 10,000 years with minimal maintenance and interruption. The full-scale clock has gone from design, to engineering, to fabrication of parts and is now under construction inside a mountain in western Texas.

Unlike most clocks that tick at one-second intervals, the *10,000 Year Clock* ticks once *per year* and has a century hand that advances once every *100 years* with a cuckoo that comes out at every millennium, or 1,000 years.

Most people aren't likely to live to see even a 100-year tick.

According to the website:

"Why would anyone build a Clock inside a mountain with the hope that it will ring for 10,000 years? Part of the answer: just so people will ask this question, and having asked it, prompt themselves to conjure with notions of generations and millennia. If you have a Clock ticking for 10,000 years, what kinds of generational-scale questions and projects will it suggest? If a Clock can keep going for ten millennia, shouldn't we make sure our civilization does as well? If the Clock keeps going after we are personally long dead, why not attempt other projects that require future generations to finish? The larger question is, as virologist Jonas Salk once asked, 'Are we being good ancestors?'"

And in Hillis' own words:

"I can't imagine the future, but I care about it. I know I am a part of a story that starts long before I can remember and continues long beyond when anyone will remember me. I sense that I am alive at a time of important change, and I feel a responsibility to make sure that the change comes out well. I plant my acorns knowing that I will never live to harvest the oaks."[16]

Be a "Good Ancestor" to Your Business' Future Owners and Employees

With so much pressure being exerted on quarterly earnings and monthly sales targets, it can be easy for companies to fall prey to their own mini-version of a short-term crisis. Most business is set up this way, with lines of credit vulnerable to being called if a short-term metric falls below a certain level. Or the value of a publicly-traded stock plummets because earnings-per-share missed Wall Street's quarterly expectations by a penny.

While it is certainly understandable to measure progress both in the short- and long-term, it also begs the question of whether we have let "made-up" time periods, such as monthly quotas or quarterly earnings, have too much of an impact on how we build our businesses.

What does the *10,000 Year Clock* have to do with Bezos or Amazon? Jeff Bezos is also, arguably, the master of long-term thinking.

Bezos owns the property in Texas where the first full-scale version of the clock is being housed. He invested $42 million to build and place the clock. He is also active in designing the "full experience of the Clock," according to the organization's website.

But the *10,000 Year Clock* is not just some vanity project funded by a guy with more money than he knows what to do with. In an interview with Dylan Tweney17, which was posted on Wired.com in 2011:

"For Bezos, the founder of Amazon.com, the clock is not just the ultimate prestige timepiece. It's a symbol of the power of long-term thinking. His hope is that building it will change the way humanity thinks about time, encouraging our distant descendants to take a longer view than we have. For starters, Bezos himself is taking a far, far longer view than most Fortune 500 CEOs."

As Bezos explained to Tweney:

"Over the lifetime of this clock, the United States won't exist. Whole civilizations will rise and fall. New systems of government will be invented. You can't imagine the world—no one can—that we're trying to get this clock to pass through."

For those of us in business, the *10,000 Year Clock* is more than just an interesting anecdote of perspective, engineering, and a $42 million passion project. The purpose of the project almost begs us to consider whether the way we operate our businesses makes us good ancestors to the shareholders and employees who will come long after our biological clocks stop ticking.

I couldn't help but wonder how business owners might adopt some of the same long-term thinking principles. Fortunately, Bezos provides some of those answers and perspectives in the Shareholder Letters, particularly the first letter he wrote in 1998 reflecting on 1997.

Long-Term Thinking and the Shareholder Letters

The Shareholder Letters are littered with references to how foundational long-term thinking is to Bezos and how committed he is to provide long-term value to Amazon investors, even if it costs the company in the short-term.

In his seminal 1997 Letter to Shareholders, for example, Bezos penned a full section about the fundamental nature of long-term thinking as the measure of success.

In the section titled "It's All About the Long Term," Bezos emphasized that growing long-term value should be the "fundamental measure" of Amazon's success. In other words, while investors might watch their quarterly earnings statements, to Bezos, they are secondary. His time and attention are much more focused on the long term.

Thinking long-term is a core tenet of Bezos and has infused the mindset and culture at Amazon since the beginning of its existence. This is as true today as it was when Bezos first started. He didn't just talk about long-term thinking when Amazon was still a corporate infant and looking to attract investment capital in 1997. If anything, the Shareholder Letters and Amazon's corporate maneuvers today evidence an even bigger focus on long-term thinking.

Bucking Wall Street—Amazon Set the Example for Apple

Amazon may be one of the very few companies that has been able to buck the Wall Street trend of quarterly earnings and focus on long-term vision and goals. But the pressure to focus on quarterly earnings is strong. Bezos started out with a long-term mindset; Apple is also trying to shift to a long-term mindset. Starting out with a long-term view, like Bezos did, is much easier than shifting mid-stream. But Bezos' example does provide evidence that a long-term approach can work.

For example, in a December 2018 *Wall Street Journal* column titled "For Companies, It Can Be Hard to Think Long Term," John

Stoll writes, "Businesses have a tough choice to make: They want to implement strategies that may take years to pay off, but Wall Street doesn't always react too kindly." He went on to note how brutally investors reacted when Apple Inc. announced they would end "its practice of reporting quarterly sales numbers for individual units," because "a 90-day performance for Macs or iPhones isn't a proxy for the underlying strength of product lines."[18]

How did investors react to Apple's decision to buck Wall Street's obsession with quarterly numbers? Its shares dropped 6.6 percent the day of the announcement, November 2, 2018, losing $71.19 billion in value from the company's market cap.

To put the drop in perspective, that one-day drop in market cap was bigger than the entire market cap of each of Biogen Idec, Inc. ($71.17 billion), Kraft Heinz Co. ($67.18 billion), Charles Schwab Corp. ($66.4 billion), FedEx Corporation ($63.45 billion), and several other S&P 500 companies, as of September 30, 2018.[19]

In other words, any one of those companies could have been wiped off the face of the planet on that day, and it *still* would not have had as much of an impact on the S&P 500 as Apple's decision to focus on the long-term when it comes to reporting sales of individual products. Stoll called Apple's decision "the latest wrinkle in the showdown between short-term and long-term thinking on Wall Street."

Wall Street just doesn't like long-term thinking. But Bezos does, so much so that he set the expectation of long-term thinking for Amazon and in the process became one of the very few companies to successfully ignore quarterly stock prices and earnings from the beginning—even during hard times like the dot-com bust when Amazon was being called names like "Amazon.bomb" and "Amazon.toast" (detractors may now be rethinking their positions on Amazon).

Amazon is willing to buck the trend, too, sacrificing this year's profits to invest in long-term customer loyalty and product opportunities that will create bigger profits next year and for years after that.

Long-term thinking allows Amazon to focus on metrics that matter. In Amazon's case, those metrics are customers and revenue growth. Investing in—and improving—the customer experience increases repeat purchases and the strength of the company's brand.

Bezos even implores potential investors to avoid investing in Amazon if their investment philosophy is inconsistent with long-term thinking. And he did so right in the 1997 Letter to Shareholders, written at a time when most startup companies were virtually begging for investors. Not Bezos. Attracting investors wasn't as important as focusing on the long term.

Or, as he puts it,

"...we want to share with you our fundamental management and decision-making approach so that you, our shareholders, may confirm that it is consistent with your investment philosophy." —Bezos (1997 Letter)

This mindset flies in the face of traditional Wall Street expectations for a public company. Bezos doesn't really care. He remains focused on the long-term growth of the business over short-term, next quarter earnings.

Think Long-Term Even When the World Rewards Short-Term Thinking

For companies that have fallen into the routine of short-term thinking, the transition to longer-term thinking could be a painful one. If you are publicly traded, you could experience similar pushback to what Apple experienced. But the sooner (and smaller) you start the transition, the sooner you will shed the internal pressure that every end-of-month quota or quarterly reporting brings from investors and analysts.

Apple really is a good example. Their stated reason for stopping reporting quarterly sales on an individual product basis was because it wasn't an accurate measure of the health of each product. I suspect for years they loyally followed what Wall Street wanted while believing deep down that it wasn't an accurate measure. It consumed time and energy, unnecessarily if you were to ask them. Imagine how frustrating and distracting it was for Apple to see the value of the company fluctuate based on a metric that the people who knew the business best believed to be irrelevant.

As I noted, staying long-term focused hasn't always been easy for Amazon either. At the turn of the century, in 2000, Bezos wrote a brutally honest letter to shareholders, which again reflects his unwavering focus on long-term thinking.

"To our shareholders:

Ouch. It's been a brutal year for many in the capital markets and certainly for Amazon.com shareholders.

As of this writing, our shares are down more than 80% from when I wrote you last year. Nevertheless, by almost any measure, Amazon.com the company is in a stronger position now than at any time in its past.

- We served 20 million customers in 2000, up from 14 million in 1999.
- Sales grew to $2.76 billion in 2000 from $1.64 billion in 1999.
- Pro forma operating loss shrank to 6% of sales in Q4 2000, from 26% of sales in Q4 1999.

- Pro forma operating loss in the U.S. shrank to 2% of sales in Q4 2000, from 24% of sales in Q4 1999.
- Average spend per customer in 2000 was $134, up 19%.
- Gross profit grew to $656 million in 2000, from $291 million in 1999, up 125%.
- Almost 36% of Q4 2000 U.S. customers purchased from one of our "non-BMV" stores such as electronics, tools, and kitchen.
- International sales grew to $381 million in 2000, from $168 million in 1999.
- We helped our partner Toysrus.com sell more than $125 million of toys and video games in Q4 2000.
- We ended 2000 with cash and marketable securities of $1.1 billion, up from $706 million at the end of 1999, thanks to our early 2000 euroconvert financing.
- And, most importantly, our heads-down focus on the customer was reflected in a score of 84 on the American Customer Satisfaction Index. We are told this is the highest score ever recorded for a service company in any industry.

So, if the company is better positioned today than it was a year ago, why is the stock price so much lower than it was a year ago? As the famed investor Benjamin Graham said, "In the short term, the stock market is a voting machine; in the long term, it's a weighing machine." Clearly there was a lot of voting going on in the boom year of '99—and much less weighing. We're a company that wants to be weighed, and over time, we will be—over the long term, all companies are. In the meantime, we have our heads down working to build a heavier and heavier company."

***

Now imagine throwing off the burden of short-term thinking for the freedom of focusing on the long-term. Think about the *10,000 Year Clock*, a clock that ticks but once per year. What decisions can you make in your company that will position it to be stronger three, seven, or 100 years from now?

Most of us can't imagine building something lasting 10,000 years. But the challenge of doing so shifts the way we think. In Amazon's case, the 1997 Letter clearly delineates Bezos' long-term approach to management and decision-making:

- We will continue to focus relentlessly on our customers.

- We will continue to make investment decisions in light of long-term market leadership considerations rather than short-term profitability considerations or short-term Wall Street reactions.

- We will continue to measure our programs and the effectiveness of our investments analytically, to jettison those that do not provide acceptable returns, and to step up our investment in those that work best. We will continue to learn from both our successes and our failures.

- We will make bold rather than timid investment decisions where we see a sufficient probability of gaining market leadership advantages. Some of these investments will pay off, others will not, and we will have learned another valuable lesson in either case.

- When forced to choose between optimizing the appearance of our GAAP accounting and maximizing the present value of future cash flows, we'll take the cash flows.

- We will share our strategic thought processes with you when we make bold choices (to the extent competitive pressures allow), so that you may evaluate for yourselves whether we are making rational long-term leadership investments.

- We will work hard to spend wisely and maintain our lean culture. We understand the importance of continually reinforcing a cost-conscious culture, particularly in a business incurring net losses.

- We will balance our focus on growth with emphasis on long-term profitability and capital management. At this stage, we choose to prioritize growth because we believe that scale is central to achieving the potential of our business model.

- We will continue to focus on hiring and retaining versatile and talented employees and continue to weight their compensation to stock options rather than cash. We know our success will be largely affected by our ability to attract and retain a motivated employee base, each of whom must think like, and therefore must actually be, an owner.

Having advised thousands of companies over more than three decades, I'd suggest these ideas could apply to businesses of all shapes and sizes with, at most, slight adjustments for unique circumstances. But the core principles can apply to *any* company, a hidden-in-plain-sight growth lesson for companies looking to build their business like Amazon.

APPLICATION

Apply Long-Term Thinking

Q: Do you have a list of long-term (and *longer*-term) goals for your company—both financial goals and strategic goals?

Q: Is your team rewarded only on quarterly or even annual performance without any reward for actions that will only pay off over the long term?

Q: How can you change short-term rewards to encourage long-term thinking?

For more resources, go to TheBezosLetters.com

Chapter Six

Principle 6:
Understand Your Flywheel

"We have invested and will continue to invest aggressively to **expand and leverage** our customer base, brand, and infrastructure as we move to establish an enduring franchise." —Bezos (1997 Letter)

"Marketplace is great for customers because it adds unique selection, and it's great for sellers—there are over 70,000 entrepreneurs with sales of more than $100,000 a year selling on Amazon, and they've created over 600,000 new jobs. With FBA, that **flywheel spins faster** because sellers' inventory becomes Prime-eligible—Prime becomes more valuable for members, and sellers sell more."—Bezos (2015 Letter)

In his bestselling book *Good to Great,* author Jim Collins used a mechanical device called a "flywheel" to demonstrate why some companies excel while others don't. The analogy plays on the connection between the physics of mechanical flywheels and what makes companies build and maintain momentum.

In an article about flywheels and business written for *Inc.,* Jeff Haden said,

"The premise of the flywheel is simple. A flywheel is an incredibly heavy wheel that takes huge effort to push. Keep pushing and the flywheel builds momentum. Keep pushing and eventually it starts to help turn itself and generate its own momentum—and that's when a company goes from good to great."[20]

For an overly-simplified illustration of a flywheel, think of how revolving doors work in large buildings. When you enter a stopped revolving door, it can take *a lot* of effort to get it moving. Children and smaller adults sometimes need to push with all their bodyweight just to get the revolving doors to start spinning.

But once they're moving and gaining momentum, it takes significantly less effort to keep them moving. Even small children can typically keep revolving doors moving with very little effort; a feat they often demonstrate by spinning around and around and flinging back out the same way they came in.

This same dynamic is the core of Collins' flywheel principle.

In business, think of your "flywheel" as a gear with spokes all around it. Each spoke on the gear is something that adds force to spin the flywheel—a key business activity that builds momentum as you move your business where you want to go. When you do more of those things, force gets applied to your flywheel and it will eventually start to turn, building momentum for your company and making it harder to stop.

The essence of the flywheel concept is that companies need to first understand the direction they want to go. Then, they need to understand what activities are so aligned with their goal that they can be spokes on the same flywheel. To be spokes on the same flywheel, the activities need to all be pushing in the same direction.

For example, on a personal flywheel, diet and exercise could be two spokes on a weight loss flywheel. The more you diet and exercise, the faster your weight loss flywheel turns. The more momentum you build on a weight loss program, the harder it will be to stop you from continuing to lose weight.

Building your business within the framework of your flywheel encourages companies to think long-term and filter activities through its bigger flywheel goals. Otherwise, you could waste time and money on activities that might be profitable in the short-term but don't help you build or keep your core momentum going.

Shortly before Collins published *Good to Great* in 2001, Bezos invited Collins to Amazon to help him understand Amazon's flywheel and identify what activities helped its flywheel turn. Here is what Amazon's flywheel looked like.

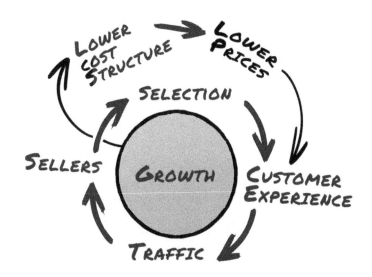

As you see, growth was identified as the company's primary goal—right in the center of the flywheel. The activities on the outside of the flywheel were the six things Amazon identified that turn its flywheel. In other words, if Amazon consistently improved these six areas, it would consistently apply pressure to its flywheel (and it didn't matter where you started):

1. Greater selection and convenience
2. Customer experience
3. Traffic to its website
4. Number of sellers
5. Lower cost structure
6. Lower prices

That original sketch showed that lower prices led to more customer visits. More customers increased the volume of sales and attracted more commission-paying third-party sellers to the site. That allowed Amazon to get more out of fixed costs like fulfillment centers and the servers needed to run the website. This greater efficiency then enabled it to lower prices further. Make any part of this flywheel go faster, and it will accelerate the entire loop leading to faster growth.

The Amazon flywheel (also known as "The Virtuous Cycle," where a complex chain of events reinforces itself through a feedback loop) defined what inputs were needed to accelerate growth–and that flywheel remains virtually unchanged today.

Amazon became a shining example of how the power of understanding your flywheel allows companies to build momentum and resist distractions; even the 2017 Whole Foods acquisition fits well within Amazon's flywheel. Look at how Amazon's CFO, Brian Olsavsky, explained the Whole Foods acquisition on an Amazon earnings call.

"I will say we do see a lot of opportunity with Whole Foods. As I said, there'll be a lot of work together between Prime Now, AmazonFresh, Whole Foods, Whole Foods products on the Amazon site, Amazon Lockers at the Whole Foods stores. So, there'll be a lot of integration, a lot of touch points and a lot of working together as we go forward. And we think we'll be also developing new store formats and everything else just as we talked about in the past before Whole Foods: Amazon Books stores, Amazon Go, and the opportunity that that technology presents. We have on-campus bookstores.

"So, we are experimenting with a lot of formats. I think that Whole Foods really gives us a vast head start on that and a great base. And a great team to work with who has a lot of history—they probably have 10 to 20 years of learning that we don't have and wouldn't have. So, we're really excited about that and I think working together, will bring our different strengths to the table and really be able to build on behalf of customers."[21]

You don't have to look very far to see how the Whole Foods acquisition helped Amazon add even more force to turn its growth flywheel even faster.

Olsavsky made clear that Amazon viewed the Whole Foods acquisition as a great way to add selection to Amazon's website and provide a better Amazon delivery experience for people who don't want packages left on their doorstep by installing delivery lockers at Whole Foods locations. And Amazon did slash prices at Whole Foods—which had previously earned the familiar nickname "Whole Paycheck"—after Amazon took it over.

Another way to think of the flywheel is that it can act as "decision leverage," giving you filters through which you can evaluate where and how you focus your resources.

Using Amazon's flywheel as an example, if Amazon is presented with a profitable activity, it must first ask itself whether the opportunity will improve one or more of the six areas reflected on its flywheel. If so, the opportunity is worth evaluating further. If not, it is a distraction at best.

While the concept of a flywheel from a mechanical perspective might require us to go back to our high school physics classes, the concept in business is relatively simple: Understanding your flywheel helps you focus time and effort on activities that help you build momentum in the direction you want to go.

The more aligned the activities on your flywheel are, the more of a self-reinforcing loop you build, and the more momentum you get with each action taken as you build toward growing *faster*.

That's when, like Jim Collins says, a company really takes off and goes from good to *great*.

How Prime Benefits Were Designed to Turn Amazon's Flywheel

Another example of Amazon building its business to turn its flywheel is the growth of Amazon Prime—it started out simply and has now grown to include multiple spokes in Amazon's wheel.

Looking back from a flywheel perspective, Amazon launched Prime with unlimited fast and free shipping in 2004. Bezos was told repeatedly it was risky, but he knew it would lead to a better customer experience, attract more traffic, and add more convenience, three parts of the Amazon flywheel.

It was a big investment, but Amazon had seen positive results from the free Super Saver Shipping and knew it could create even more momentum by making shipping even more convenient for a small fee. In the 2014 Letter, Bezos shared that an analyst had predicted Amazon would be able to significantly lower its costs of fast shipping if it achieved scale.

Amazon's big bet paid off, and Amazon's flywheel—designed specifically to grow Amazon over the long term—spun faster and faster. As Amazon grew, its ability to add features to Amazon Prime members grew as well, adding music, streaming video, photo storage, the ability to borrow Kindle books, and more.

> "Notice also what happens from a Prime member's point of view. Every time a seller joins FBA [Fulfilled by Amazon], Prime members get more Prime eligible selection. The value of membership goes up. This is powerful for our flywheel. FBA completes the circle: Marketplace pumps energy into Prime, and Prime pumps energy into Marketplace." —Bezos (2014 Letter)

In other words, the original Prime features helped Amazon grow. That growth helped Amazon add *more* features to Prime. Those features added more convenience, selection, customer experience, and other benefits to subscribers. That helped the flywheel spin faster and faster, creating a reinforcing loop of benefits to Amazon and its customers.

How to Understand Your Own Flywheel

To build your own flywheel, look no further than Collins' books: the original book, *Good to Great,* and the 2019 monograph (a companion guidebook) which he called *Turning the Flywheel.*

On his website introducing the monograph, Collins asks readers to consider identifying their own flywheel by asking themselves the following questions:[22]

- How does your flywheel turn?
- What are the components in your flywheel?
- What is the sequence in your flywheel?

Your flywheel will likely look different than Amazon's. But the flywheel concept is one that works for every organization. For example, a luxury goods provider might not have "lower prices" on its flywheel; it might have greater purchasing power for quality materials, an essential component for profitability for their business.

That's why it's important to identify the things that matter in *your* organization.

When creating your own flywheel, remember, for your flywheel to work, it needs to be done with a specific goal in mind that works for your business. Amazon's flywheel was designed to help it grow. If your flywheel is also designed for growth, what causes it to turn? What are the core components? Do they work together in a sequence to potentially create a reinforcing loop?

The flywheel concept can help provide clarity and drive strategy for any business in any industry. It helps organizations understand what risks and opportunities to take and what to walk away from. Remember, as you filter your decisions through your flywheel, and focus your resources on doing things that turn your flywheel toward the goal of your business, you will gain momentum and grow like Amazon.

APPLICATION

Understand Your Flywheel

Q: What is at the center of your company's flywheel?

Q: What are the key drivers or activities that turn your flywheel?

Q: How do those drivers reinforce each other to make your flywheel spin faster?

For more resources, go to TheBezosLetters.com

Growth Cycle: Accelerate

Generate High-Velocity Decisions

Make Complexity Simple

Accelerate Time with Technology

Promote Ownership

To Amazon, accelerating is how you take something that has been tested and built and then super-charge your growth. It involves making decisions as quickly as possible to push forward with an initiative that has already been examined and focused.

It requires you to simplify everything that you can to remove any points of friction between the initiative and the market. It requires creative use of technology to move quickly.

When you've taken strategic risks and gotten answers that support moving forward (whether hardware, software, product, business expansion, or whatever) you can then harness technology to maximize your efforts.

And to achieve the most successful results, a passionate team around each initiative is a must. The process of accelerating makes Amazon an extremely fast-paced, dynamic company.

Chapter Seven

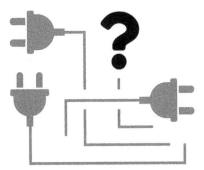

Principle 7:
Generate High-Velocity Decisions

"The senior team at Amazon is determined to keep our decision-making velocity high. Speed matters in business—plus a **high-velocity decision-making** environment is more fun too." —Bezos (2016 Letter)

Although I've never met Jeff Bezos, I think I can safely say he *loathes* wasting time.

And one area where many businesses really get bogged down is in the area of decision-making. Often, the bigger the company gets, the longer decisions take (including the less important ones).

Bezos knows you need both a *philosophy* and a *methodology* for making the decision-making process more efficient.

After testing and building, a business is primed to accelerate. However, Bezos notes, achieving meaningful growth can be stalled—or derailed—if people don't make decisions well. In his words:

"There are some subtle traps that even high-performing large organizations can fall into as a matter of course, and we'll have to learn as an institution how to guard against them. One common pitfall for large organizations—one that hurts speed and inventiveness—is 'one-size-fits-all' decision making.

"Some decisions are consequential and irreversible or nearly irreversible—one-way doors—and these decisions must be made methodically, carefully, slowly, with great deliberation and consultation. If you walk through and don't like what you see on the other side, you can't get back to where you were before. We can call these Type 1 decisions.

"But most decisions aren't like that—they are changeable, reversible—they're two-way doors. If you've made a suboptimal Type 2 decision, you don't have to live with the consequences for that long. You can reopen the door and go back through. Type 2 decisions can and should be made quickly by high judgment individuals or small groups.

"As organizations get larger, there seems to be a tendency to use the heavy-weight Type 1 decision-making process on most decisions, including many Type 2 decisions. The end result of this is slowness, unthoughtful risk aversion, failure to experiment sufficiently, and consequently diminished invention." —Bezos (2015 Letter)

Bezos' approach to decision-making starts by recognizing that you shouldn't treat all decisions the same. Doing that wastes time and increases unexpected risks. Awareness of the type of decisions you are facing is the first step to high-velocity decision-making and maximizing your Return-on-Risk.

In today's fast-paced economy, businesses don't have the luxury of "taking their time" to make decisions, like they did even a few years ago. So, the trap is set: Either a company becomes paralyzed into making *no* decisions or they rush into big decisions that expose them to unnecessary risk.

Bezos solves this by articulating two types of decisions:

1. **Type 1** decisions are major decisions with big consequences and no turning back.
2. **Type 2** decisions are ones that can be changed or reversed, and the world isn't going to come to an end.

Bezos knows most failures are not fatal and most decisions are not irreversible.

Thus, he encourages people to make decisions quickly, by recognizing that most decisions are actually Type 2 decisions. He says:

"We don't know all the answers, but here are some thoughts.

"First, never use a one-size-fits-all decision-making process. Many decisions are reversible, two-way doors. Those decisions can use a lightweight process. For those, so what if you're wrong?

"Second, most decisions should probably be made with somewhere around 70% of the information you wish you had. If you wait for 90%, in most cases you're probably being slow. Plus, either way, you need to be good at quickly recognizing and correcting bad decisions. If you're good at course correcting, being wrong may be less costly than you think, whereas being slow is going to be expensive for sure.

"Third, use the phrase 'disagree and commit.' This phrase will save a lot of time. If you have conviction on a particular direction even though there's no consensus, it's helpful to say, 'Look, I know we disagree on this but will you gamble with me on it? Disagree and commit?' By the time you're at this point, no one can know the answer for sure, and you'll probably get a quick yes." —Bezos (2016 Letter)

Again, Bezos is willing to take the risk of a decision being "wrong" for the expediency of making decisions of lesser consequence fast.

As Bezos notes, many companies slow down as they grow. And while it is natural for leaders to want to protect what they have built by making sure decisions are made carefully, they often end up doing more harm than good by treating every decision like a Type 1 decision.

What makes high-velocity decision-making possible at Amazon is that Bezos has built a company where 600,000-plus employees are empowered to act fast when facing the equivalent of Type 2 decisions.

In other words, good leaders know how to make decisions well—and at Amazon everyone is expected to be a "leader" no matter what their job or position is. They know the difference between Type 1 and Type 2 decisions. They dedicate the appropriate amount of time and effort to each decision. They feel empowered to voice their opinions and they respect the decisions of their colleagues—even when they disagree.

*"Amazon Leadership Principle—*Disagree and Commit: Leaders are obligated to respectfully challenge decisions when they disagree, even when doing so is uncomfortable or exhausting. Leaders have conviction and are tenacious. They do not compromise for the sake of social cohesion. Once a decision is determined, they commit wholly. "

The key here is that not everyone has to agree for a decision to be made at Amazon. Bezos doesn't require a unanimous vote; instead, he emphasizes commitment once a decision is made. It is a philosophy they strive to have permeate every part of their culture.

How to Accelerate Growth by Making High-Velocity Decisions

Amazon makes it clear that high-velocity decision-making starts by building a culture that accepts small failures and practices dynamic invention and innovation. Remember, the first Anderson Growth Principle states that Amazon "Encourages Successful Failure," which allows people to take smaller risks and assess what went wrong to turn them into future successes.

Amazon practices dynamic invention and innovation, which creates an environment of experimentation. It is a similar principle to the old sports adage that "the best defense is a good offense." Betting on big ideas is that "good offense" that outweighs all the little ideas that don't work out. In Amazon's case, a handful of ideas generates billions of dollars every year. And it allows people to move forward with things they are not sure will work.

How do these principles lead to high-velocity decision-making?

The culture of "successful failure" makes it easier for employees at all levels to embrace Type 2 decisions–and without constant fear of failure, employees will be free to make those decisions quickly. Meanwhile, the imperative to "practice dynamic invention and innovation" creates an environment in which team members are eager to act on ideas, rather than endlessly debate them.

"Amazon Leadership Principle—Bias for Action: Speed matters in business. Many decisions and actions are reversible and do not need extensive study. We value calculated risk-taking."

First, each leader must train their team to be able to evaluate a decision and move quickly. First, they must talk with the team about the definitions of Type 1 and Type 2 decisions.

Second, they must talk about the decision-making process for both kinds of decisions to help them delineate between the two.

Third, they must remind each team member about the greater purpose and culture the company is looking to achieve.

Type 1 decisions can be almost impossible to reverse. Bezos calls these decisions "one-way doors." Selling your company is likely a Type 1 decision. It's not easily reversible. It could be impossible. Quitting your job without another job lined up may be a Type 1 decision. Also not reversible, and there could be substantial consequences.

Type 2 decisions are typically reversible, even if it is difficult. As Bezos says, they're "two-way doors." Starting a side business to help supplement your income is easily reversible if it does not work out. For a business, it could be offering a new service or introducing new pricing structures. Each of these, if they don't work out, can be changed.

Reminding employees of the greater purpose (in Amazon's case, customer obsession) will help establish a "safe to risk" culture. This gives team members the freedom to make decisions quickly and safely.

After implementing the process to empower employees to evaluate and take action based on the type of decision, it's not uncommon to find that teams spend less money, take smaller but smarter risks, and achieve much better results. Employees who have the autonomy and clear structure to make Type 2 decisions become more effective in their jobs.

Let me be clear: I am *not* suggesting you should tolerate stupid or repeated failures.

What I am suggesting is that you have a bias toward action when the decisions are somewhat risky with limited downside.

This is what Bezos preaches and teaches to his team at Amazon. If things go wrong, learn from what went wrong so you can know how to proceed better the next time. Start slow. Let them know they will need to be able to justify their decision, but you trust them to decide what is best and work it out if they find another course of action is better.

What does Amazon do if someone abuses the process or makes the same mistakes over and over again?

Let's just say they don't tolerate incompetence.

That's why Amazon puts so much weight on hiring the *right* people. But even the right people make mistakes. All people make mistakes. Amazon knows this and wants people who know how to limit the downside of mistakes by taking smart risks. They even ask people about their "failures" during job interviews.

The truth is, the businesses that will be most successful at high-velocity decision-making know the following before they take action, even while making sure to take action as soon as possible. You need to know:

- Where you're going
- The types and amounts of risks you need to take to get there
- That risk and risk-taking are assets and investments in your future
- Taking the right amount and types of risks maximizes your Return on Risk and reduces the impact of something not working

High-velocity decision-making is a dynamic process. Each company will have a different sweet spot when it comes to the speed of decisions that are right for their culture. And within an organization, there will be sweet spots as a whole as well as "micro-level" sweet spots for individual departments or specific people.

High-velocity decision-making is not an "edict" that is issued, but an overall business growth strategy to be adopted.

If you are having trouble distinguishing between Type 1 and Type 2 decisions, think of it this way:

- Type 1 decisions are usually more *strategic,* and Type 2 decisions tend to be more *operational.*
- Type 1 decisions typically involve changing *what* you are doing, while Type 2 decisions are more often related to *how* you are doing it.

Bezos believes both are important, and everyone who works for Amazon is expected to always be on the lookout for the differences.

Each business or organization needs to define what is a Type 1 or Type 2 decision for themselves. Remember, it's about identifying which decisions are easily reversible (those are Type 2) and, when in doubt, defaulting to speed.

Bezos' Methodology: The Six-Page Narrative

One counterintuitive methodology for making high-velocity decisions at Amazon is Bezos' requirement that employees create a six-page memo before every decision-making meeting. While creating these memos (and reading them at the beginning of the meeting) slows things down, "slowing down to speed up" is actually enormously effective.

Yes, speed of decision-making is crucial. But thorough and informed decision-making is *vital* for business growth, especially when it comes to Type 1 decisions.

That's why at the other end of the high-velocity scale is Amazon's six-page narrative (a.k.a. 6-pager, 6-page memo, 6-page narrative). The six-page narrative intentionally slows down the process of making decisions.

The six-page narrative is a document created around any new idea, reflecting the thought process around it, and written in the form of a "story." It's a clear telling of the idea or project as if you were having a conversation with someone and explaining to them what's behind this new idea you have. When people talk with each other, they don't talk in bullet points. The narrative is descriptive and reads like a book, not like a pie chart. (There may be appendices with supporting data and information.)

The six-page narrative is the first step in the idea "investigation" process. It may be about creating a new product or going in a new direction or setting up a new process. But in any case, taking "risk" is not taken lightly. Each new idea is explored with great intentionality.

In fact, one of the unique characteristics of the six-page memo, true to Jeff Bezos' orientation, is that everyone is asked to project into the future. The perspective is shifted from "if this were to work" to "*when* this works, x will happen." It's a shift in mindset. Consequences are thought out beforehand, both positive and negative.

Type 1 decisions are not made on the fly. The six-page narrative process makes sure everyone is extremely well informed before the idea is approved for more testing and additional resources (if any are actually given). More often than not, the thought process required to create a six-page narrative fleshes out the idea and improves it, making sure the idea is a great one before it is given a "green light." But Amazon often requires its people to figure out how to make it happen without being given any money—creativity at its highest.

Most every meeting requires some kind of "memo"; bigger decisions may take the full six pages, but lesser decisions may just require a one- or two-page memo. The point is, you don't go into a meeting without the details being thoroughly thought through.

Literally, with the six-page memo, everyone gets on the same page, and even though a six-pager is harder for the author than putting together a few PowerPoint slides or a one-page bullet list, it forces the author to clarify their thinking.

And if the idea doesn't work out, everyone can go back to the original narrative to see what they might have missed. The six-pager creates the "brief and the debrief" at the same time.

"We don't do PowerPoint (or any other slide-oriented) presentations at Amazon. Instead, we write narratively structured six-page memos. We silently read one at the beginning of each meeting in a kind of "study hall." Not surprisingly, the quality of these memos varies widely. Some have the clarity of angels singing. They are brilliant and thoughtful and set up the meeting for high-quality discussion. Sometimes they come in at the other end of the spectrum.

"In the handstand example, it's pretty straightforward to *recognize* high standards. It wouldn't be difficult to lay out in detail the requirements of a well-executed handstand, and then you're either doing it or you're not. The writing example is very different. The difference between a great memo and an average one is much squishier. It would be extremely hard to write down the detailed requirements that make up a great memo. Nevertheless, I find that much of the time, readers react to great memos very similarly. They know it when they see it. The standard is there, and it is real, even if it's not easily describable.

"Here's what we figured out. Often, when a memo isn't great, it's not the writer's inability to *recognize* the high standard, but instead a wrong expectation on *scope*: they mistakenly believe a high-standards, six-page memo can be written in one or two days or even a few hours, when really it might take a week or more! The great memos are written and re-written, shared with colleagues who are asked to improve the work, set aside for a couple of days, and then edited again with a fresh mind. They simply can't be done in a day or two. The key point here is that you can improve results through the simple act of teaching scope—that a great memo probably should take a week or more.

"(As a side note, by tradition at Amazon, authors' names never appear on the memos—the memo is from the whole team.)" —Bezos (2017 Letter)

As Bezos pointed out, writing a six-page narrative isn't a solo effort—it's a collaborative process. The higher up you are in the organization, the more likely it is that there are other people working on the narrative with you. Typically, executives spend a week or more sharing the document with colleagues, getting feedback, and honing and tweaking it until every conceivable facet is deeply thought through. (One of the worst things that can happen to your career at Amazon is to present a poorly written narrative to an executive team.)

As an added benefit, with the amount of effort needed to create a successful six-page memo, the number of meetings that are called is cut down dramatically. Think about it—if you have to spend a week writing a memo, you don't just start sending out meeting invitations whenever the impulse strikes you. And the meetings aren't large; company policy limits attendance to only those who have a direct need to be there. (Bezos also has his "two pizza rule" where the meeting can't be larger than two large pizzas can feed.)

Each meeting starts with a thirty-minute quiet time where everyone thoroughly reads the memo. From there, all attendees are asked to share gut reactions—senior leaders typically speak last—and then delve into what might be missing, ask probing questions, and drill down into any potential issues that may arise.

"I definitely recommend the [six-page] memo over PowerPoint. And the reason we read them in the room, by the way, is because just like, you know, high school kids, executives will bluff their way through the meeting as if they've read the memo. Because we're busy. And so, you've got to actually carve out the time for the memo to get read and that's what the first half hour of the meeting is for and then everybody has actually read the memo, they're not just pretending to have read it. It's pretty effective." —2018 Forum on Leadership, "Closing Conversation with Jeff Bezos," George W. Bush Presidential Center at SMU[23]

Here's some insight into how the process works from Brad Porter, VP and Distinguished Engineer, Robotics at Amazon:

"Imagine for a moment that you could go into a meeting and everyone in the meeting would have very deep context on the topic you're going to discuss. They would be well-versed in the critical data for your business. Imagine if everyone understood the core tenets you operate by and internalized how you're applying them to your decisions.

"How great would it be not to be constantly interrupted by clarifying questions? How great would it be not to have the decisions in the meeting based on the social networking advocacy that happened before the meeting? How great would it be if executives deeply understood your organization from your perspective before asserting they know better how to do it? How great would it be to be able to review the core data going into a decision rather than have someone summarize it and assert that correlation is causality without revealing their work?

"This is what meetings are like at Amazon and it is magical."[24]

Components of the Six-Page Narrative

Sandy Carter, VP of Amazon Web Services, talked about the six-page memo in an online presentation. She was new to Amazon and had to learn how to write and structure the memo. This is her list of items that can/should be included (comments in the parentheses are mine):

Steps to Create a Six-Page Narrative

1. Write the Press Release (This is the press release you would release in the future when the project is launched that tells the world about the project and why it's important.)

2. Write the FAQs (Answer the common questions people will ask, in advance.)

3. Define the User Interaction (Explain how it works.)

4. Write the Manual (Give instructions on how it works.)

5. Answer these Questions:
   - Who is the customer?
   - What is the customer problem or opportunity?
   - What is the most important (singular) customer benefit? (Choose only one benefit, but make sure it's the most significant one.)
   - How do you know what the customer needs? (Support the origin of the project.)
   - What does the customer experience look like? (Anticipate how the customer will react and respond.)

Why Does This Methodology Work So Well for Amazon?

Amazon's method of slowing down by requiring six-page memos for bigger decisions and speeding up by making quicker, lower-risk decisions has been an undoubted success. It helps Amazon, as a whole, go forward much faster over the long term. But why?

For one thing, the narrative format of the six-page memo forces the author to think things through and present their idea in a story format, which better engages the readers at the meeting. Most would agree that our brains are wired to appreciate and understand stories differently than raw information. Ultimately, the purpose of the memo is always to communicate the idea well and ensure it is implemented with appropriate intent and careful consideration regarding how the idea fits into Amazon's flywheel.

Also, when *everyone* is empowered to make Type 2 high-velocity decisions (the ones that don't have irreversible consequences), those making the Type 1 heavy-consequence decisions are freed up to focus on what matters most in the bigger picture.

As Bezos has said, one of the pitfalls of larger organizations is they aren't nimble–and the bigger the company gets, the longer decisions take (including the less important ones).

The bottom line: Slow-velocity decision-making makes high-velocity decision-making possible, and vice versa.

This full-circle decision-making process is what helps accelerate Amazon's growth and continues the momentum on their flywheel.

***

Note: There is only one occasion where Bezos has referenced a separate document he wanted shareowners to read, and that was in his 2005 Letter. Obviously, he found it important enough to include.

In his note he says,

"The Structure of 'Unstructured' Decision Processes is a fascinating 1976 paper by Henry Mintzberg, Duru Raisinghani, and Andre Theoret. They look at how institutions make strategic, 'unstructured' decisions as opposed to more quantifiable 'operating' decisions. Among other gems you will find in the paper is this: **'Excessive attention by management scientists to operating decisions may well cause organizations to pursue inappropriate courses of action more efficiently.'** They are not debating the importance of rigorous and quantitative analysis, but only noting that it gets a lopsided amount of study and attention, probably because of the very fact that it is more quantifiable. The whole paper is available at www.amazon.com/ir/mintzberg." —Bezos (2005 Letter)

APPLICATION

Generate High-Velocity Decisions

Q: Do you have a mechanism for distinguishing between Type 1 and Type 2 decisions—and does everyone on your team understand the difference?

Q: Do you have a system in place for making Type 1 decisions well? (What's your version of the six-page memo?)

Q: Do you have a mechanism in place for making Type 2 decisions fast?

For more resources, go to TheBezosLetters.com

Chapter Eight

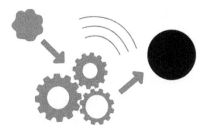

Principle 8:
Make Complexity Simple

"...Kindle makes it more convenient for readers to buy more books. Anytime you make something **simpler and lower friction,** you get more of it." —Bezos (2007 Letter)

On Christmas Eve this past year, my wife and I gathered with our daughter, her husband, and four of our (adorable) grandchildren, ages five, three, eighteen months, and a newborn, at their home in Pittsburgh. My son-in-law's extended family also came over, so there were quite a few presents to open. By the end of the night, trucks, dinosaurs, books, puzzles, and wrapping paper littered the floor. But amidst all the fun, the adults were struggling with scissors and pocket knives to remove many of the toys from their "childproof" hard plastic clamshell packaging.

The kids were eagerly waiting for toys to play with while the adults were anxiously trying to pry them open without poking an eye out or slicing open their fingers. Even though it was a fun time, it was stressful just trying to get the toys from their packages—except for the toys from Amazon, which were delivered in Frustration-Free Packaging.

Why do most product manufacturers refuse to do something about their customers' packaging frustrations?

Two primary reasons are that the packaging on the shelves helps sell the products (visibility) and packaging protects that product until someone buys it. Getting the product out of the packaging isn't the manufacturer's "problem"; they really only need to ensure the product is visible and the customer gets an intact product.

For toys, in particular, being able to see a perfectly-positioned superhero or beautiful princess is appealing to children when their parents are shopping the aisles. (Parents are often left to choose between temper tantrums and taking the toy home. I admit, as a parent, I have on occasion chosen the latter.)

But Amazon doesn't have shelves or aisles. It has *listings.*

Amazon doesn't need perfectly-positioned products. It has pictures, videos, descriptions, and customer reviews to sell products. It doesn't have aisles for customers to go up and down, it has product listings to scroll up and down, and unlimited space for images and videos.

In the beginning, when customers bought from Amazon instead of a brick and mortar retail store, they got the frustration of trying to open a package that was designed for traditional retail outlets without needing the benefits of traditional packaging.

So, in 2008, Bezos and his team decided it was time to do something about it: they decided to eliminate that frustration of a complex "traditional way of doing things" and replace it with a more efficient (and simple) way to package products.

Coined "Frustration-Free Packaging," the idea was for Amazon to work with product manufacturers to create special "Amazon-only" packaging for items sold on Amazon. The packaging would need to be easy to open and recyclable. No twists. No scissors. No elastics. No frustration. No tears. No blood.

The idea allowed customers to choose whether they wanted traditional packaging or the Frustration-Free Packaging. So, if you ordered something as a gift and wanted to ensure the recipient knew the product was new, you could select traditional packaging at checkout. If you didn't have a reason to prefer traditional packaging, you could choose Frustration-Free Packaging and enjoy a happier holiday or birthday party.

If you have experienced anything similar to what we did last Christmas, Frustration-Free Packaging might seem like a no-brainer. But what makes it a no-brainer for Amazon is that the service closely aligns with Amazon's typical customer journey—online ordering that's easy and hassle-free.

Solving customer frustrations pays off.

Within five years, Amazon's Frustration-Free Packaging program had become a hit. Here is how Bezos described the program's genesis and growth over the first five years:

"Our battle against annoying wire ties and plastic clamshells rages on. An initiative that began five years ago with a simple idea that you shouldn't have to risk bodily injury opening your new electronics or toys, has now grown to over 200,000 products, all available in easy-to-open, recyclable packaging designed to alleviate 'wrap rage' and help the planet by reducing packaging waste.

"We have over 2,000 manufacturers in our Frustration-Free Packaging program, including Fisher-Price, Mattel, Unilever, Belkin, Victorinox

Swiss Army, Logitech, and many more. We've now shipped many millions of Frustration-Free items to 175 countries. We are also reducing waste for customers—eliminating 33 million pounds of excess packaging to date.

"This program is a perfect example of a missionary team staying heads-down focused on serving customers. Through hard work and perseverance, an idea that started with only 19 products is now available on hundreds of thousands and benefiting millions of customers." — Bezos (2013 Letter)

As you can see, the main focus of the Frustration-Free Packaging program was alleviating one of the biggest customer irritations. And I have to admit, the toys that came from Amazon that were in the Frustration-Free Packaging were exactly that—frustration-free.

More and more product manufacturers are catching on that their old-style packaging, which was conceived to help products stand out among hundreds of others on shelves in a physical store, isn't working for customers who want their items delivered to their front door.

Amazon touts that its Frustration-Free Packaging is more sustainable, right-sized, and made of recyclable materials. Packaging is designed to be easier to open and even to reduce damage to products during shipping. It's better for Amazon, it's better for the customer, and it's better for the Earth. They have made something complex simple. It's a win-win-win.

Creating the Kindle to Simplify Book Collections and Portability

If you pull back the curtain behind e-readers, the Kindle is a testament to making complexity simple... well, simple for the user.

The late Everett Rogers defined *skunkworks* as an "enriched environment that is intended to help a small group of individuals design a new idea by escaping routine organizational procedures."[25]

If Amazon had a skunkworks program it was Lab126, which was created to develop hardware (a shift for Amazon into developing physical products). Its first success: an electronic book reader that became known as the Amazon Kindle.

The Amazon Kindle dominated the 2007 Letter to Shareowners. Bezos begins,

"November 19, 2007, was a special day. After three years of work, we introduced Amazon Kindle to our customers.

"Many of you may already know something of Kindle—we're fortunate (and grateful) that it has been broadly written and talked about. Briefly, Kindle is a purpose-built reading device with wireless access to more than 110,000 books, blogs, magazines, and newspapers. The wireless connectivity isn't WiFi—instead it uses the same wireless network as advanced cell phones, which means it works when you're at home in bed or out and moving around. You can buy a book directly from the device, and the whole book will be downloaded wirelessly, ready for reading, in less than 60 seconds. There is no 'wireless plan,' no year-long contract you must commit to, and no monthly service fee. It has a paper-like electronic-ink display that's easy to read even in bright daylight. Folks who see the display for the first time do a double-take. It's thinner and lighter than a paperback, and can hold 200 books. Take a look at the Kindle detail page on Amazon.com to see what customers think—Kindle has already been reviewed more than 2,000 times.

"As you might expect after three years of work, we had sincere hopes that Kindle would be well received, but we did not expect the level of demand that actually materialized. We sold out in the first 5½ hours, and our supply chain and manufacturing teams have had to scramble to increase production capacity.

"We started by setting ourselves the admittedly audacious goal of improving upon the physical book. We did not choose that goal lightly. Anything that has persisted in roughly the same form and resisted change for 500 years is unlikely to be improved easily. At the beginning of our design process, we identified what we believe is the book's most important feature. It *disappears*. When you read a book, you don't notice the paper and the ink and the glue and the stitching. All of that dissolves, and what remains is the author's world.

"We knew Kindle would have to *get out of the way*, just like a physical book, so readers could become engrossed in the words and forget they're reading on a device. We also knew we shouldn't try to copy every last feature of a book—we could never out-book the book. We'd have to add *new* capabilities—ones that could never be possible with a traditional book.

"I'll highlight a few of the useful features we built into Kindle that go beyond what you could ever do with a physical book. If you come across a word you don't recognize, you can look it up easily. You can search your books. Your margin notes and underlinings are stored on the server-side in the 'cloud,' where they can't be lost. Kindle keeps your place in each of the books you're reading, automatically. If your eyes are tired, you can change the font size. Most important is the seamless, simple ability to find a book and have it in 60 seconds. When I've watched people do this for the first time, it's clear the capability has a profound effect on them. Our vision for Kindle is every book ever printed in any language, all available in less than 60 seconds." —Bezos (2007 Letter)

At the launch of the Kindle in November 2007, the store had more than 88,000 digital titles available. An impressive amount, to be sure. But now, there are *millions* of books available on Kindle.

Amazon would go on to build an entire ecosystem around the Kindle e-reader.

Whispersync is the Kindle service provided by Amazon designed to ensure that everywhere you go, no matter what devices you have with you, you can access your reading library and all of your highlights, notes, and bookmarks, all in sync across your Kindle devices and mobile apps. (Audiobooks were added later and includes Audible so you can be listening to a book and seamlessly transfer to reading it.)

> "The technical challenge is making this a reality for millions of Kindle owners, with hundreds of millions of books, and hundreds of device types, living in over 100 countries around the world—at 24x7 reliability. At the heart of Whispersync is an eventually consistent replicated data store, with application defined conflict resolution that must and can deal with device isolation lasting weeks or longer. As a Kindle customer, of course, we hide all this technology from you. So, when you open your Kindle, it's in sync and on the right page. To paraphrase Arthur C. Clarke, like any sufficiently advanced technology, it's indistinguishable from magic." —Bezos (2010 Letter)

Creating the Echo and Alexa to Make Daily Life Simpler

Amazon started with the Kindle, but over time their inventive Lab126 continued their efforts to make the complex simple.

I have no doubt that when he was presented with the concept, the idea of what's now known simply as "Alexa" was super-exciting to Jeff Bezos.

Over fifty years ago, in 1966 (when Jeff Bezos would have been around two years old), a science fiction TV show debuted called *Star Trek.* In this space fantasy world, the USS Starship *Enterprise* computer responded to voice commands, and handheld devices were used for communication.

Many of the fictional ideas from *Star Trek* have come true. The crew used handheld "communicators," and Apple certainly came through with the concept when they launched the iPhone (even though the Amazon Fire Phone was a great try).

And then there is Alexa. Like the voice-activated computer on the USS *Enterprise*, Alexa is machine-learning speech recognition software that powers the Echo hardware device. The power of Alexa (and the Echo) is the combination of a hardware device that listens for a "wake word" and then the software responds to audio commands and questions.

Creating a speech recognition system that could match Google or Apple was a complicated task—especially considering the huge head start those companies had from building their smartphone software. But Amazon has now risen to the top of voice control with the Echo and Alexa.

(One of the engineering marvels of the Echo devices is the quality of the far field voice recognition. Far field means you can literally stand ten to fifteen feet from the device, say the trigger word, and wake up the device to respond.)

The original vision for the Echo did not include connecting it to other internet-enabled devices (IoT, or Internet of Things) including light bulbs and thermostats made by other companies. On a lark, an engineer rigged the speaker to work as a voice controller for a streaming TV device. When Bezos saw it, it was a "forehead-slapping moment." (This is one of those situations where people can try something new and see what happens. Needless to say, Bezos was probably elated with this particular "on a lark" experiment.)

The impact of the Echo (Alexa) has been influenced heavily by the development of the Internet of Things (IoT)—devices that include everything from your bedroom lights to your refrigerator door shopping list can now be operated by voice commands. The Echo speaker can serve as a hub for a myriad of "smart home" devices that are flooding the market.

Some of us may remember the cartoon comedy series *The Jetsons* that foretold life in a future century with robot servants, flying saucer-like cars, and moving sidewalks to walk the dog. We don't have flying cars (yet) but, thanks to Alexa, many of the Jetsons' home voice commands are becoming commonplace today.

Similar to Apple in its early years, Amazon opened the Echo platform to third-party developers. By the end of 2018, there were more than 70,000 Skills available on Echo devices worldwide. (Skills are Amazon's name for third-party software programs that create voice controls that consumers can use.)

The success of the Amazon Echo is in some ways a result of the "successful failure" of the Fire Phone. Once Amazon killed off its "shopping phone," they could focus more resources on voice control efforts and what they had learned in the process. Now, Alexa is managing our lights, our shopping, our schedules, and more.

The next big task for Alexa may be making dinner… and that may not be as far-fetched as it sounds.

Self-Service Checkout and Amazon Go

"I am emphasizing the self-service nature of these platforms because it's important for a reason I think is somewhat non-obvious: even well-meaning gatekeepers slow innovation. When a platform is self-service, even the improbable ideas can get tried, because there's no expert gatekeeper ready to say, 'that will never work!' And guess what—many of those improbable ideas do work, and society is the beneficiary of that diversity." —Bezos (2011 Letter)

Self-checkout systems have been available in various retail stores like grocery stores, warehouse stores, and home improvement stores for quite some time. The advantage to customers is not having to wait in a long line to pay for your items. The disadvantage is self-checkouts don't always work very well.

I have a love-hate relationship with self-checkout. You may have experienced the same frustration I have of scanning items and putting them in the bagging area only to have the automated voice tell you "unexpected item in bagging area," a legitimate need by the retailer to prevent you from taking an item without having paid for it but one that causes friction for the customer. Or you also can get the dreaded "attendant notified" message indicating you are stuck until the attendant can come and manually reset the machine.

And it's not much better when you're standing in line waiting for a cashier to scan your items, even the "10 items or less" line. I always feel like I've gotten in the "wrong line" and someone invariably needs a price check or some other matter that needs assistance—and even though it may only take a few moments, it always feels like it takes forever.

My experience shopping at one of the new *Amazon Go* convenience stores was a completely different (and pretty awesome) experience.

After checking into my hotel in Chicago, I walked a few blocks to the recently opened Amazon Go convenience store located on the ground floor of an office building.

Turnstile gates prevented me from entering the store until I scanned the barcode from the Amazon Go app on my phone that's connected to my Amazon account. Once the barcode was scanned, the doors opened, and I entered the store and began to walk around.

There were shelves with various prepared food items including sandwiches, salads, fresh fruit, and typical convenience store items such as chips and various types of drinks. To shop, you simply take an item off the shelf and put it into your basket. I grabbed some lunch and a coffee mug for Karen that said *Just Walk Out Shopping* and headed for the exit, fighting the inclination to find a place to pay.

Because at Amazon Go, once you've finished your shopping, you "just walk out." That's it. Done.

I felt like I hadn't paid, but in fact, I had. A few minutes later I received an email and a notification through my app with the receipt for my purchases. It got it exactly right.

What a different experience it is to shop in the Amazon Go store with "just walk out shopping" instead of the often-frustrating experience using the self-checkout in a traditional retail store.

The Amazon Go store concept is an example of the implications of Amazon's "customer obsession" toward making the complex simple. They are always focused on what is best for their customer.

"For many years, we considered how we might serve customers in physical stores, but felt we needed first to invent something that would really delight customers in that environment. With Amazon Go, we had a clear vision. Get rid of the worst thing about physical retail: checkout lines. No one likes to wait in line. Instead, we imagined a store where you could walk in, pick up what you wanted, and leave.

"Getting there was hard. Technically hard. It required the efforts of hundreds of smart, dedicated computer scientists and engineers around the world. We had to design and build our own proprietary cameras and shelves and invent new computer vision algorithms, including the ability to stitch together imagery from hundreds of cooperating cameras. And we had to do it in a way where the technology worked so well that it simply receded into the background, invisible. The reward has been the response from customers, who've described the experience of shopping at Amazon Go as 'magical.'" —Bezos (2018 Letter)

When Amazon says, "just walk out," they mean it.

Using Alexa Skill Blueprints

Would it be helpful to be able to have your overnight houseguests ask Alexa for your current WiFi password? Would you like to leave Alexa with a set of instructions for your babysitter (or pet sitter) when you've gone out for the evening? How amazing would it be for your teenagers to ask Alexa for a list of daily chores they have to accomplish before they can go out for the evening with friends?

All this is possible using Alexa Skill Blueprints.

Alexa Skill Blueprints are ways you can customize Alexa simply and easily without having to be a programmer or techie. They're as simple as downloading an app on your phone.

Blueprints are fill in the blank templates that walk you through the process of setting up a Skill and one of the latest initiatives Amazon is taking to make your life easier.

There are even Alexa Skill Blueprints for business that enable companies to create custom Skills, and none of this requires writing code. Amazon offers dozens of preconfigured templates along with a wizard-like process that walks you through making a Skill. Once the Skill is finished, the platform creates a way for the company to "approve" the Skill using the IT department or someone else. When the Skill is accepted, it can then be rolled out companywide.

Amazon has used technology to "speed up time" for customers.

Blueprints are examples of several of the 14 Growth Principles including "obsess over customers" and "make complexity simple." The continued development of the Alexa voice ecosystem gives a picture of how important Amazon considers this new Skill Blueprint endeavor. It may be another initiative on Amazon's part that may be considered deceptive in its beginning stages.

There are many who may be underestimating the role of Amazon's AI (Artificial Intelligence) as it creates new and faster technologies for the marketplace. Alexa Skill Blueprints may end up being another "hockey stick" success for Amazon—and others who are paying attention.

A Start to Making Complexity Simple in Health Care

In June 2018, Amazon purchased PillPack, an online pharmacy company, for a reported $1 billion. PillPack's unique market position was that it makes taking multiple prescription medications simpler by delivering them in pre-sorted doses. Essentially, they deliver people's prescriptions in single-dose packs. PillPack's service is free to consumers, just like a regular pharmacy.

All users pay is their copay and anything else they order that is not covered by an insurance plan, such as vitamins or over-the-counter medications. PillPack takes care of the insurance, prescription transfer, and coordinating refills. Its target market is someone taking five or more medications a day who has a hard time keeping track of what medications to take and when (which is a growing population in the Boomer generation).

With Amazon's reputation for reliable service, PillPack's "make medications simple" promise was a big pill to swallow—pun intended— in the drugstore industry. In fact, the day the acquisition was announced, major drugstore chains, such as Walgreens, CVS Health, and Rite Aid, collectively lost $11 billion in stock value.

Notwithstanding the significant drop in stock prices, Stefano Pessina, CEO of Walgreens Boots Alliance, said he was "not particularly worried" about the Amazon/PillPack deal when asked about it on an earnings call. "The pharmacy world is much more complex than just delivering certain pills or certain packages. I strongly believe that the role of the physical pharmacy will continue to be very, very important in the future."[26]

Of course, his comment might be wishful thinking. Because that's what Amazon does: they make complexity simple.

APPLICATION

Make Complexity Simple

Q: What are the biggest "barriers to entry" for new customers to doing business with you?

Q: What can you do to make it easier for existing customers to increase their business with you?

Q: What's the most complicated or complex part of your customer's experience with you—and how can you simplify it?

For more resources, go to TheBezosLetters.com

Chapter Nine

Principle 9: Accelerate Time with Technology

"Invention is in our DNA and **technology is the fundamental tool** we wield to evolve and improve every aspect of the experience we provide our customers. We still have a lot to learn, and I expect and hope we'll continue to have so much fun learning it. I take great pride in being part of this team." —Bezos (2010 Letter)

If you've ever built a fire, you know the effect of adding fuel to your fire. Putting lighter fluid on a charcoal grill makes the fire accelerate.

When asked what a good *business* accelerant is, I suspect most businesses might say "more money" or "more employees" would be their key to faster growth. But Jeff Bezos knows that what makes Amazon more successful than others is—in part—how technology accelerates the speed (and time) in which the company can grow.

Why Accelerating Time with Technology Is Easier Than Ever

Virtually all information is being digitized. Companies that digitize are at a significant advantage. They can analyze more information. They can access information faster. They can have more reliable, and up-to-date, data.

In the not too distant past, it took years and millions of dollars or more to launch an industry-shaking business. The cost to take an idea and create a company has dropped dramatically. Today, $5,000 (or less) will get you started. Like the mainframe computer that took up whole rooms in the early days of computing, the computing power we have now in our smartphones has exceeded most people's wildest dreams.

New startups are able to use cloud platforms to access computing power that would have been unimaginable twenty years ago at a fraction of the cost. Because of that, business moves faster than ever, and business cycles have gone from years or decades to months or shorter.

Technology is a time accelerant that is only going to continue to gain speed.

Crises hit fast. Competition comes fast. New technology will come faster and harder, and if you don't have a plan for using it to your advantage, some other company will use it for theirs. Right now, companies around the world are trying to make your business irrelevant and, eventually, someone will succeed in doing that if you don't take action to secure your position in the marketplace.

Amazon has figured out how to stay nimble as they've grown to be one of the largest companies in the world—I believe by how they harness the power of technology.

The only way you can ensure your company won't become irrelevant is through smart risk-taking and innovation.

Businesses don't have the same amount of time today than they did, even a few years ago, to evaluate the risks and opportunities they face because ***not doing something*** is a bigger risk than doing something.

In other words, *in*action is as big a problem as action.

How to Use Technology to "Accelerate Time"

You may have watched a professional sports game and heard the announcer talk about the game "speeding up" on some of the players and the game "slowing down" for others. While time doesn't literally speed up or slow down for those players, the reference refers to the ability of some players to stay calm and focused and make good decisions when the stakes are highest.

That same phenomenon happens in business all the time. When companies take control and get intentional with their growth, they end up like the player for whom time seems to slow down. They move fast but don't feel rushed. They feel in control.

The best way to control your accelerant and "speed up" or "slow down" time is to be very intentional about how you use technology to accelerate your growth.

Bezos identified early that technology would continue to improve, and Amazon could take advantage of those improvements to increase customer satisfaction. (Remember, that's why he started Amazon in the first place—he saw the statistic that the internet was growing at a rate of 2,300 percent a year and he sensed that kind of growth would generate huge business opportunities. His risk paid off.)

Having been in the tech world for the last thirty-five-plus years, I have seen a "hockey stick" curve in technology. Bezos applies *exponential technologies* to grow Amazon's business. He is constantly looking for opportunities to use technology to innovate Amazon's existing practices to make the business grow faster and better. A great example is the development of Amazon Web Services.

The truth is, with technology changing so rapidly, if you sit back and don't do anything, it's only a matter of time (probably shorter than you think) before someone else uses technology to make part—or all—of your business obsolete. The better way is for *you* to be the one to use technology to make part—or all—of your business obsolete. Which means you're always on the cutting edge.

That's what Amazon is always doing. When you are the one looking for new ways to invent, innovate, and harness technology, you take the lead.

Exponential Growth

When a new technology, process, or platform digitizes information, it enters an exponential growth stage. Because the early parts of exponential growth are hard to detect, the impact of technology can be very "deceptive," a term for how technology can be misleading. It may appear that a technology will go nowhere or will not have wide appeal but, again, that can be deceptive.

Here's a simple illustration. Take a penny and double it every day. For a couple weeks, the amount of money is inconsequential; by day 18 you only have a little over $1,200. Yet at a certain point, the hockey stick curve that is an indicator of exponential growth becomes apparent.

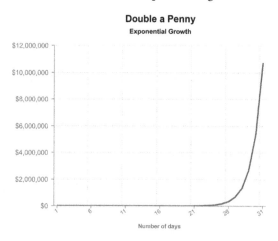

Double a Penny
Exponential Growth

By the end of thirty-one days, you will have over $10 million. It's only in the last few days where the doubling has such a significant impact.

So, the early stages of exponential growth are very deceptive. Time may seem like it's slow, but it's building speed, nonetheless.

Often the thought of the upfront cost to adopt a technology doesn't seem worth it. But it may be that it's possible that the technology is at the beginning of an exponential growth cycle.

AWS and the Seven-Year Lead

When creating Amazon Web Services (cloud computing), Amazon was essentially creating their own internal Internet Operating System (IOS) and then leveraging their technology infrastructure into a profit center. He said,

> "IT departments are recognizing that when they adopt AWS, they get more done. They spend less time on low value-add activities like managing datacenters, networking, operating system patches, capacity planning, database scaling, and so on and so on. Just as important, they get access to powerful APIs [Application Programing Interfaces] and tools that dramatically simplify building scalable, secure, robust, high-performance systems. And those APIs and tools are continuously and seamlessly upgraded behind the scenes, without customer effort."
> —Bezos (2014 Letter)

In other words, Amazon took the proprietary infrastructure they built for themselves and turned it into a service that any developer could use for their own purposes.

It took some time for AWS to take hold, but today it's a highly lucrative business generating *significant* profits for Amazon. In fact, Bezos said,

"At AWS, we completely reinvented the way that companies buy computation. Then a business miracle happened. This never happens. This is like the greatest piece of business luck in the history of business so far as I know. We faced no like-minded competition for seven years. It's unbelievable. When I launched Amazon.com in 1995, Barnes & Noble launched Barnesandnoble.com in 1997. Two years. That's very typical, if you invent something new. We launched Kindle, Barnes & Noble launched Nook two years later, we launched Echo, Google launched Google Home two years later.

"When you pioneer, if you're lucky, you get a two-year head start. Nobody gets a seven-year head start! And so that was incredible because I think it was a whole confluence of things. I think that the big established enterprise software companies did not see Amazon as a credible enterprise software company. And so, we had this long runway to build this incredible little feature-rich [service], and it's just so far ahead of all the other products and services available to do this work today." —2018 Interview, *The David Rubenstein Show*, Bloomberg

"It's exciting to see Amazon Web Services, a $20 billion revenue run rate business, accelerate its already healthy growth. AWS has also accelerated its pace of innovation—especially in new areas such as machine learning and artificial intelligence, Internet of Things, and serverless computing. In 2017, AWS announced more than 1,400 significant services and features, including Amazon SageMaker, which radically changes the accessibility and ease of use for everyday developers to build sophisticated machine learning models." —Bezos (2017 Letter)

"All of a Sudden It Was Here"

At some point along the process, the exponential growth that technological advancements facilitate becomes "disruptive." All of a sudden, people are noticing the new technology.

It seems to many people that the technology came out of nowhere. If you were paying attention to the "deceptive" stage, however, you would have had a better idea of the potential impact. There are numerous examples of technology and platforms becoming disruptive. The easy ones to talk about are Uber and Airbnb. Yet, there are many others that created connecting platforms that would change entire industries.

The disruption doesn't always come at an industry-wide level, such as what Uber did to the taxi industry. It could disrupt a part of your business, giving the companies who adopt that technology a competitive advantage over the others. Bezos is always on the lookout for disruptive technology on both the industry-wide and competitive-balance perspectives.

At Amazon, technology permeates their teams, their processes, their decision-making, and their approach to innovation in each of their businesses. It is deeply ingrained into everything they do.

For any business, the continued adoption and adaptation of technology improves the customer experience, which feeds the business flywheel, accelerating the whole business as it turns.

Google, Microsoft, and many others are working hard to catch up.

Fulfillment Centers

Kids love to see how things are made. There's something fascinating about looking at all the parts and seeing the various pieces come together and actually make something that works. Even as an adult, I'll take any opportunity to go on a factory tour.

I scheduled an appointment to tour Amazon's Jeffersonville, Indiana, fulfillment center. Amazon doesn't allow picture taking within the fulfillment centers and makes everyone keep their cell phones in their pockets, so unfortunately, I was left taking a visual inventory of my tour.

The Jeffersonville Fulfillment Center is a soft goods fulfillment center, which means a large amount of their inventory is apparel and soft goods, such as jewelry and other clothing accessories. Once the group gathered, our first stop was a training room where we watched a short video about Amazon. We were then given a headset so we could hear the tour guide describe what we were seeing. The fulfillment center was a busy, loud industrial warehouse; it employs almost 2,500 people during the regular season and more than 6,000 people during peak seasons. It houses more than thirty million items in about 2.5 million square feet of usable space.

In a fascinating turn of events, the tour followed products backward in their journey through the warehouse. So, we started at the point where they ship out to the customer and ended at the arrival from the manufacturer into the fulfillment center.

Flipping the timeline from the end to the beginning made for an incredible experience, especially as it related to my research for this book. Until that point, like many people, my experience with Amazon's products had been mostly as a consumer. I'd place my order online and my order would show up at my door. Thus, starting the tour at the end, when products ship to consumers, made the experience feel more like I was tracing the products backward from the consumer's perspective.

The technology used by Amazon at the fulfillment center was remarkable. An extensive conveyor system throughout the warehouse shuttled products at high speeds. If the warehouse didn't have the right-size box for the item, it didn't miss a beat. Someone grabs any box that would fit the item because the program is designed to get the product out as fast as possible.

If you've ever wondered why the package you received from Amazon may be oversized for the item, that's the reason. They don't care about boxes. *They care about getting the items out.* Sophisticated automation is evident everywhere. Before the boxes dash along the conveyor belts, packers pick the items out of big yellow bins and pack them into boxes. Along the way, a shipping label is automatically applied. It's a fascinating process to watch.

Before the items are packed, they are stored on storage shelves in what seems to be a completely random order. Items are literally stored on *any* shelf where there's an empty space. This means a particular storage bin could have five completely different items stored next to each other. (This warehouse storage technique is called chaotic storage, a term I wish I knew when my parents used to tell me to clean my room as a child.)

It's estimated that Amazon can store 25 percent more inventory in the same space than traditional warehouses using technology to more than make up for the perceived inefficiency of a chaotic storage system.

When a customer clicks an order, a picker—a *human*—with a handheld computer and a cart with a yellow bin gets a notification. The computer tells the picker exactly where to go to find the items ordered. The picker gets the items, scans them, and places them into the yellow bin. Once all the items available at that fulfillment center are picked, the storage bin is placed on a conveyor and sent to the packing station.

(As a side note, Amazon's latest generation of fulfillment centers are incorporating robotics where, instead of the picker going to the shelf, a robot will bring the shelf to the picker. Experimenting with efficiency is another way to look at accelerating time with technology.)

The last stop on the tour was the other end of the warehouse where at least twenty loading docks were unloading material coming into the warehouse. Incoming products included those sold directly by Amazon as well as those from Amazon Marketplace sellers and Fulfilled by

Amazon sellers. Each incoming box is scanned and inspected. If there are any problems with the packaging or if the barcode doesn't match the expected product, the box is set aside for manual processing.

The technology being used by Amazon to move faster and more efficiently was impressive. Since 2012, after its acquisition of Kiva Systems, Amazon has used robotics, artificial intelligence, and automation to grow its storage capacity and allow its warehouses to support higher sales volume. Amazon currently has 175 fulfillment centers in operation around the globe.[27] It has already outfitted twenty-five of those centers with robots to supplement human workers.

APPLICATION

Accelerate Time with Technology

Q: How are you using technology to speed up your business growth?

Q: In what way could you use technology to make part of your business obsolete (before your competitor does it for you)?

For more resources, go to TheBezosLetters.com

Chapter Ten

Principle 10: Promote Ownership

"Once again this year, I attach a copy of our original 1997 letter and encourage current and prospective share**owners** to take a look at it."
—Bezos (2002 Letter)

In what appeared to be a throwaway five-word sentence in the 2002 Letter to Shareowners, Bezos summarized a key principle that has been a core part of Amazon's growth. "Owners are different from tenants."

"Long-term thinking is both a requirement and an outcome of true ownership. Owners are different from tenants. I know of a couple who rented out their house, and the family who moved in nailed their Christmas tree to the hardwood floors instead of using a tree stand.

Expedient, I suppose, and admittedly these were particularly bad
tenants, but no owner would be so short-sighted." —Bezos (2003 Letter)

The tenants *nailed the Christmas tree directly into the hardwood
floors.* If you have ever owned rental property, that anecdote might
seem distressingly familiar. As Bezos notes, "no owner would be so
shortsighted."

Since I travel frequently for business, I get rental cars a lot. Even
with something as simple as leaving trash in the car when I turn it in, I
have to confess on occasion thinking "it's a rental." I wouldn't do that
with my own car. And that's why I'm always reluctant to purchase a
rental vehicle. I know I don't always care for a rental car like I do my
own car, and I know I'm hardly the worst offender.

The same is true with investing. Bezos continues,

"Similarly, many investors are effectively short-term tenants, turning
their portfolios so quickly they are really just renting the stocks that
they temporarily 'own.'" —Bezos (2003 Letter)

In other words, ownership is a mindset. When someone acts like an
owner of something, they think of it differently and treat it more like
their own. This is markedly different from a renter's mindset.

Taking Ownership

Owners truly are different than tenants, but what does that mean
for your business? And how did that concept become so integral to
Amazon and its growth?

In the original 1997 Letter Bezos explained,

"We will continue to focus on hiring and retaining versatile and talented
employees and continue to weight their compensation to stock options

rather than cash. We know our success will be largely affected by our ability to attract and retain a motivated employee base, each of whom must think like, and therefore must actually be, an owner."—Bezos (1997 Letter)

Taking ownership of your work isn't a unique concept; people in business frequently complain about team members not taking enough ownership of their work. But, once again, Bezos and his team at Amazon take "ownership" to an entirely different level.

Instead of encouraging people to take ownership of their work, Amazon asks their team members to actually *think like owners of the company.* It is one of Amazon's key Leadership Principles for the whole company, too:

*"Amazon Leadership Principle—***Ownership:** Leaders are owners. They think long-term and don't sacrifice long-term value for short-term results. They act on behalf of the entire company, beyond just their own team. They never say 'that's not my job.'"

Bezos wants *everyone* involved with the company to think like owners—frontline employees to senior-level executives. Owners think about the long-term implications and impact of decisions, not just on short-term quarterly earnings or quick wins that don't have lasting value. This allows Amazon to evaluate their team members based on whether they are acting like owners—people who don't say, "Not my problem." Thinking like an owner is a key mindset developed and encouraged in the Amazon culture.

In the 2002 Letter, Bezos started using the term "share*owners*" instead of "share*holders*" when referring to Amazon's investors. In essence, investors really do "own" a part of Amazon, and they should feel like owners and not tenants who have no interest in the company and only want financial gain.

He reinforced his belief by changing his opening from "To our shareholders" to "To our shareowners" in 2007 and has continued to use that opening ever since.

Clearly this concept of having an owner mindset, and truly considering yourself an owner, is one of the keys to creating a culture that will continue to grow over time.

How to Promote Ownership

So, how does Bezos promote ownership? Here are a few ways:

Addressing people as owners. One of the simple but effective ways he promotes the concept is through language. By changing "shareholders" to "shareowners," he reinforces what he believes is a fundamental tenet for Amazon—investors are not outsiders but insiders.

Giving employees stock in the company. When employees are given stock, they are more likely to feel invested and have personal ownership.

> "One of the ways we foster ownership among employees is through Restricted Stock Unit (RSU) awards. RSUs are a key part of our global compensation program, which has been carefully designed to help us attract, motivate and retain employees of the highest caliber. An RSU is a right to receive a share of Amazon.com common stock after you've worked for the company for a certain amount of time and met other service conditions." —*Amazon Restricted Stock Units: Becoming an Owner*[28]

Decision-making. Done the Amazon way, employees are empowered to make Type 2 decisions. When an employee is able to make a decision on behalf of the company, particularly to help a customer, they are likely to feel empowered—a vital way to connect with the values of the company.

Meetings. Again, done the Amazon way, meetings reinforce "common cause" for the company; using the six-page narrative format gives people the ability to connect as a team and work together on a common goal or idea, thus promoting ownership.

Creating opportunity to invent and innovate. At Amazon, inventing and innovation is *assumed*. Everyone is expected to be on the lookout for how to make things better, especially while they're on the clock.

Encouraging leadership. Leadership is *expected* and everyone is given a copy of the Amazon Leadership Principles when they come to work at Amazon. They get support from Amazon to live them out. And it's "real" support, not just lip service. (This is not to say they are 100 percent successful, just that this is what they aspire to.)

Giving the opportunity to "opt out." Employees are there because they *want* to be.

> *"Pay to Quit* ... was invented by the clever people at Zappos, and the Amazon fulfillment centers have been iterating on it. Pay to Quit is pretty simple. Once a year, we offer to pay our associates to quit. The first year the offer is made, it's for $2,000. Then it goes up one thousand dollars a year until it reaches $5,000. The headline on the offer is 'Please Don't Take This Offer.' We hope they don't take the offer; we want them to stay. Why do we make this offer? The goal is to encourage folks to take a moment and think about what they really want. In the long-run, an employee staying somewhere they don't want to be isn't healthy for the employee or the company."—Bezos (2013 Letter)

Not requiring total agreement for everything. To make that happen, Amazon has a "disagree and commit" system for employees, including Bezos. The idea is that everyone won't agree on a given decision, but it's still possible for people who disagree to work toward the same goal—they are all in it for the common goal: what's best for the customer.

Bezos mentioned not being sure about a proposed Amazon Prime television series, partly because of his level of interest in it, and partly because of the business terms of the deal. He said:

> "They had a completely different opinion and wanted to go ahead. I wrote back right away with 'I disagree and commit and hope it becomes the most watched thing we've ever made.' Consider how much slower this decision cycle would have been if the team had actually had to *convince* me rather than simply get my commitment." —Bezos (2016 Letter)

Customers Can Feel "Ownership" Too—Amazon Smile

My wife and I met in high school through Young Life, a faith-based outreach to students. We have continued to support Young Life financially through the years and just recently rotated off the Board of Young Life Capernaum, an outreach to students with disabilities. We were both pleased when we learned about the *Amazon Smile* program where Amazon would donate a small percentage of each sale to the charity of our choice. We elected to support Young Life through our purchases on Amazon Smile.

In fact, since we each have our own Amazon accounts, we have a little competition to see who's giving the most money through our purchases. (My guess is, she'll win.)

> "In 2013 we launched Amazon Smile—a simple way for customers to support their favorite charitable organizations every time they shop. When you shop at smile.amazon.com, Amazon donates a portion of the purchase price to the charity of your choice. You'll find the same selection, prices, shipping options, and Prime eligibility on smile.amazon.com as

you do on Amazon.com—you'll even find your same shopping cart and wish lists. In addition to the large, national charities you would expect, you can also designate your local children's hospital, your school's PTA, or practically any other cause you might like. There are almost a million charities to choose from. I hope you'll find your favorite on the list." — Bezos (2013 Letter)

Being able to support a charity of our choice goes a long way toward giving us a feeling of connection with Amazon. We don't own any stock in the company (hindsight is 20/20) but having a portion of our dollars spent going to a cause we support helps us feel like we are making a difference.

Is this ownership? Maybe, maybe not.

But does it make us feel like we're working together with Amazon to do something good?

Absolutely.

APPLICATION

Promote Ownership

Q: Do you offer any compensation to your team in the form of company "ownership"—including a share of profits or growth?

Q: Do you regularly communicate to your team your short-term goals and your long-term goals for the business?

Q: Is there an incentive (or a barrier) for employees to improve or fix areas of the business outside of their own department or responsibilities?

For more resources, go to TheBezosLetters.com

Growth Cycle: Scale

Maintain Your Culture

Focus on High Standards

Measure What Matters,
Question What's
Measured, and
Trust Your Gut

Believe It's
Always Day 1

To Amazon, scaling is how you achieve tremendous growth without sacrificing who you are or what you offer. It requires creating and maintaining an innovative culture—a culture that's willing to take risk on behalf of the customer.

It involves a committed focus on maintaining high standards and not sacrificing quality to achieve greater profitability. It involves measuring only what matters and continuously questioning what you measure to make sure you are always focused on the right metrics—but not ignoring your intuition in the process.

And, finally, it requires you to always—above all things—make decisions as if it is your first day in business, with passion and focus on customers. Be lean, be focused, and remember what mattered on Day 1 still matters.

Scaling makes Amazon able to come full circle—to leverage its successes and begin again the process of testing another offering.

Chapter Eleven

Principle 11: Maintain Your Culture

"...we are working to build something important, something that matters." —Bezos (1997 Letter)

"We never claim that our approach is the right one—**just that it's ours**—and over the last two decades, we've collected a large group of like-minded people. Folks who find our approach energizing and meaningful." —Bezos (2015 Letter)

"We challenge ourselves to not only invent outward facing features, but also to find better ways to do things internally—things that will both make us more effective and benefit our thousands of employees around the world." —Bezos (2013 Letter)

There are lots of stories out there about what it's like to work for Amazon. And there's probably a bell-shaped curve at work—some people love working there, some people hate working there, and most people are somewhere in the middle.

But there are some interesting ways to look at the culture of Amazon from the outside. Two of those are through LinkedIn and the *Wall Street Journal*/Drucker Institute. LinkedIn looks at overall employee satisfaction and retention, and *WSJ*/Drucker Institute looks at overall management.

The 2019 LinkedIn Top Companies list revealed the fifty companies where Americans want to work—and stick around once they're in. Alphabet (Google), Facebook, and Amazon were the top three.

In its post, LinkedIn said, "Every year, our editors and data scientists parse billions of actions taken by LinkedIn members around the world to uncover the companies that are attracting the most attention from jobseekers and then hanging onto that talent. The data-driven approach looks at what members are doing—not just saying—in their search for fulfilling careers."[29]

The *Wall Street Journal* publishes an annual list of the Management Top 250 companies in cooperation with, and compiled by, the Drucker Institute, ranking the most effectively run major U.S. public companies.

The rankings are made up of thirty-seven indicators that fall under five dimensions of performance: customer satisfaction, employee engagement and development, innovation, social responsibility, and financial strength. These ideas represent core values of management expert Peter Drucker, who wrote more than thirty business books over his long career.

In 2017, Amazon was number one on the list for the Best Run Company in the U.S. and number two in 2018, being beaten out for the top spot by Apple. And Amazon's score for innovation topped every other company by a wide margin.

How has Amazon maintained its culture as it has scaled from a few employees to over 600,000 and growing?

Amazon has done many things to maintain its culture, but two stand out: its focus on personal leadership and its corporate focus on constant and continuous growth.

In his annual Letter to Shareowners, Bezos reminds everyone that it is always Day 1. In the Bush Center interview at the SMU (Southern Methodist University) campus, when asked about Day 1 (given the exponential growth Amazon has had with over 600,000 employees and growing), Bezos quickly reframed the question, stating,

"So, the real question for me is, how do you go about **maintaining** a Day 1 culture?

"It's great to have the scale of Amazon, we have financial resources, we have lots of brilliant people. We can accomplish great things. We have global scope; we have operations all over the world. But the downside of that is that you can lose your nimbleness, you can lose your entrepreneurial spirit, you can lose that kind of heart that small companies often have. And so, if you could have the best of both worlds, if you could have that entrepreneurial spirit and heart, while at the same time having all the advantages that come with scale and scope—think of the things that you could do.

"So, the question is how do you achieve that? The scale is good because it makes you robust. A big boxer can take a punch to the head. You also want to dodge those punches. So, you'd like to be nimble; you want to be big and nimble. I find there are a lot of things that are protective of the Day 1 mentality. I already spent some time on one of them, which is customer obsession. I think that's the most important thing.

"It gets harder as you get bigger. When you're a little tiny company, say you're a ten-person startup company, every single person in the company is focused on the customer. When you get to be a bigger company, you've got middle managers, and you've got all these layers. And those people aren't on the front lines. They're not interacting with customers every day. They're insulated from customers, and they start to manage not the customer happiness directly, but they start to manage through proxies like metrics and processes. And, some of those things can become bureaucratic. So, it's very challenging.

"But one of the things that happens is the decision-making velocity slows down. And I think one of the reasons that happens is that people, junior executives inside the big company, start to model all decisions as if they are heavyweight, irreversible, highly consequential decisions. And like two-way doors, if you make a decision, and it's the wrong decision, you can just back up, back through the door, and try again. But even those reversible decisions start to be made with heavyweight processes.

"And so, you can teach people [about] these pitfalls and traps and then teach them to avoid those traps. And that's what we're trying to do at Amazon so that we can maintain our inventiveness and our heart and our kind of small company spirit, even as we have this scale and scope of a larger company." —2018 Forum on Leadership, "Closing Conversation with Jeff Bezos"

In that context, employees are reminded of what Day 1 means through the Amazon Leadership Principles, which define what Amazon expects from each and every employee, including Bezos. They define how each employee is to treat each other. They also define how each employee is to treat Amazon's partners and customers.

Amazon's Day 1 culture and mindset can be felt throughout the organization. It can be observed through what Bezos says in the Letters, how Amazon maneuvers in the marketplace, and through the Amazon Leadership Principles.

14 Amazon Leadership Principles

"We use our Leadership Principles every day, whether we're discussing ideas for new projects or deciding on the best approach to solving a problem. It is just one of the things that makes Amazon peculiar [a word used by Bezos and most Amazonians]."[30]

Customer Obsession: Leaders start with the customer and work backwards. They work vigorously to earn and keep customer trust. Although leaders pay attention to competitors, they obsess over customers.

Ownership: Leaders are owners. They think long term and don't sacrifice long-term value for short-term results. They act on behalf of the entire company, beyond just their own team. They never say "that's not my job."

Invent and Simplify: Leaders expect and require innovation and invention from their teams and always find ways to simplify. They are externally aware, look for new ideas from everywhere, and are not limited by "not invented here." As we do new things, we accept that we may be misunderstood for long periods of time.

Are Right, A Lot: Leaders are right a lot. They have strong judgment and good instincts. They seek diverse perspectives and work to disconfirm their beliefs.

Learn and Be Curious: Leaders are never done learning and always seek to improve themselves. They are curious about new possibilities and act to explore them.

Hire and Develop the Best: Leaders raise the performance bar with every hire and promotion. They recognize exceptional talent, and willingly move them throughout the organization. Leaders develop leaders and take seriously their role in coaching others. We work on behalf of our people to invent mechanisms for development like Career Choice.

Insist on the Highest Standards: Leaders have relentlessly high standards—many people may think these standards are unreasonably high. Leaders are continually raising the bar and drive their teams to deliver high quality products, services, and processes. Leaders ensure that defects do not get sent down the line and that problems are fixed so they stay fixed.

Think Big: Thinking small is a self-fulfilling prophecy. Leaders create and communicate a bold direction that inspires results. They think differently and look around corners for ways to serve customers.

Bias for Action: Speed matters in business. Many decisions and actions are reversible and do not need extensive study. We value calculated risk taking.

Frugality: Accomplish more with less. Constraints breed resourcefulness, self-sufficiency and invention. There are no extra points for growing headcount, budget size or fixed expense.

Earn Trust: Leaders listen attentively, speak candidly, and treat others respectfully. They are vocally self-critical, even when doing so is awkward or embarrassing. Leaders don't believe their or their team's body odor smells of perfume. They benchmark themselves and their teams against the best.

Dive Deep: Leaders operate at all levels, stay connected to the details, audit frequently, and are skeptical when metrics and anecdote differ. No task is beneath them.

Have Backbone; Disagree and Commit: Leaders are obligated to respectfully challenge decisions when they disagree, even when doing so is uncomfortable or exhausting. Leaders have conviction and are tenacious. They do not compromise for the sake of social cohesion. Once a decision is determined, they commit wholly.

Deliver Results: Leaders focus on the key inputs for their business and deliver them with the right quality and in a timely fashion. Despite setbacks, they rise to the occasion and never settle.

Inward Innovations: An Approach to Building and Keeping a Workforce

One of the other big areas of innovation at Amazon is the way Amazon builds its workforce, which Bezos refers to as "inward innovations." Three inward innovations illustrate Amazon's workplace culture: Career Choice, Pay to Quit, and Virtual Contact Center.

Amazon is also at the forefront of continuing education for its team, implementing a program called **Career Choice**, where it prepays 95 percent of tuition for employees to take courses for in-demand fields, such as airplane mechanic or nursing, regardless of whether the skills are relevant to a career at Amazon.

For some, Amazon will be their long-term career of choice. For others, Amazon recognizes it might be a stepping-stone on the way to a job somewhere else and they might need new skills to get that job. Amazon is more than willing to help them attain those skills, even if another company will benefit from Amazon's investment in education.

While Amazon's claim of being okay with paying for people to train for jobs at other companies sounds altruistic—and it very well might be—a side benefit for Amazon is the type of workforce that program would encourage. Specifically, if people don't want to be at Amazon, they have ways to leave. If they are taking advantage of the program, they are incentivized to work hard and perform well while at Amazon to not lose the tremendous opportunity of a paid-for education. It is an innovative—albeit counterintuitive—way to build a strong workforce.

Pay to Quit is an example of another counterintuitive program that Amazon supports. Though it came originally from Zappos with Amazon's acquisition of that company, Bezos touts it as a favorite way to build a strong workforce. Again, as he says in the 2013 Letter,

> "The goal is to encourage folks to take a moment and think about what they really want. In the long-run, an employee staying somewhere they don't want to be isn't healthy for the employee or the company." — Bezos (2013 Letter)

Virtual Contact Center allows employees to provide customer service support for certain products from home. As Bezos puts it,

> "This flexibility is ideal for many employees who, perhaps because they have young children or for another reason, either cannot or prefer not to work outside the home." —Bezos (2013 Letter)

These "inward innovations" allow Amazon to build a workforce full of people who want to be there, rather than people who *have* to be there.

The Benefits of Remembering the "Early Days"

In 1995, when Amazon had five employees, Bezos needed to find a creative solution for most everything. He had borrowed $300,000 from his parents and had to make every penny count.

The employees of the fledgling business needed desks for their offices. When walking through the neighborhood Home Depot, Bezos realized he could make simple desks by adding legs to solid core doors a lot cheaper than buying desks. Four 4x4s to use as legs, braces to connect the legs to the desktop, and a few screws and voila!—Jeff Bezos created the Amazon "door desk." (If you're curious, Amazon has instructions on how to make a door desk on their company blog.)[31]

While the "door desk" was a necessity in 1995, thousands of employees still use "door desks" to this day, although more modern versions than the makeshift ones Amazon used in 1995. These modern versions pay tribute to and remind each employee that it is always Day 1 every time they sit at their desk. (Bezos still uses a "door desk," but after twenty-plus years, it seems the original one didn't stand the test of time.)

Early Amazon employee Nico Lovejoy described what the "door desk" represents on Amazon's company blog—unsurprisingly called the "Day One" blog. "I think it represents ingenuity, creativity and peculiarity, and the willingness to go your own path."[32]

For Amazon, savings are more than a corporate competitive matter. Indeed, the company holds "frugality" up as one of Amazon's Leadership Principles as it "breeds resourcefulness, self-sufficiency and invention."

In an interview with CBS's Bob Simon for *60 Minutes,* Bezos connected frugality to his #1 rule: Think about the customers' needs *first.* "It's a symbol of spending money on things that matter to customers and not spending money on things that don't," Bezos explained to Simon.[33]

The company still hands out the "Door Desk Award," a title given internally to select employees who have a "well-built idea" that creates a significant savings for the company and enables lower prices for customers.

It's not just blog names and door desks that keeps the Day 1 mentality visible, either.

When Amazon grew to occupy its own office building in Seattle, Bezos named the building "Day 1." On the side, Bezos added a placard[34] reminding everyone who enters the building of the founding Day 1 principle from the 1997 Letter to Shareholders:

> "There's so much stuff that has yet to be invented. There's so much new that's going to happen. People don't have any idea yet how impactful the Internet is going to be and that this is still Day 1 in such a big way."
> —Bezos (1997 Letter)

While it might seem subtle or even silly, most business owners know the value of repetition in forming corporate culture and influencing behavior. These visible cues of the Day 1 mentality do much more than pay homage to Amazon's corporate history. They give visual reminders of what is important to Amazon from a culture perspective.

They also present opportunities for Amazon employees to discuss what Day 1 means with each other and outsiders. When a new person comes to Amazon, if they don't know already, they might ask why so many people use doors as desks. When a new vendor comes to the Day 1 building, they might ask about the building's name or read the placard on the side. Each time an employee, vendor, investor or visitor asks such a question, it creates an opportunity for the Day 1 mentality to be reinforced in the mind of the person answering.

We can all create our own visual cues, incorporating parts of our history into things our team members use every day. However we do it, those cues will help cultivate a culture like the one Nico Lovejoy described of ingenuity, creativity, peculiarity, and the willingness to go your own path.

But door desks can also be a symbol of innovation and a reminder to not just be frugal, but creative.

In several conversations I had with former Amazonians, one of the cultural distinctives at Amazon is the ability for virtually any employee to come up with an idea, pitch it to their manager, and if the idea is good enough, receive permission to experiment to validate the premise. If it works, the idea will be implemented throughout the unit, team, group, or division. Amazon's culture is one where everyone has a chance to innovate and see innovations through to implementation.

"Like any company, we have a corporate culture formed not only by our intentions but also as a result of our history. For Amazon, that history is fairly fresh and, fortunately, it includes several examples of tiny seeds growing into big trees. We have many people at our company who have watched multiple $10 million seeds turn into billion dollar businesses. That first-hand experience and the culture that has grown up around those successes is, in my opinion, a big part of why we can start businesses from scratch. The culture demands that these new businesses be high potential and that they be innovative and differentiated, but it doesn't demand that they be large on the day that they are born." —Bezos (2006 Letter)

One more reason for Amazon's top innovation score from the *Wall Street Journal*/Drucker Institute study is their focus on creating small teams and the creative power that is harnessed through small team cooperation.

Bezos doesn't like big and long meetings, nor does he like huge teams. When a meeting is absolutely necessary, he has a rule that boosts their productivity. Again, he calls it the "two pizza rule"—the meeting can't be any bigger than can be fed by two large pizzas.

When you contrast that with other large corporations that use a more bureaucratic structure that can stifle creativity and innovation, it's easy to see why Amazon keeps coming out on top.

So how did Amazon grow from just Bezos and a few developers to 647,500 employees and maintain their "peculiar" culture?

I believe one of the biggest reasons is they have tried to be intentional about not letting success "go to their heads." As I said in the beginning, Amazon is not a perfect company. But obviously, they are doing something right.

They have maintained their culture through using the Amazon Leadership Principles with every employee (whether frontline worker or senior executive), and they have many corporate cues and reminders that help them remember their focus on Bezos' highest value—to be customer *obsessed.*

They continue to innovate even though they hit $100 billion… because to have long-term growth in business, you have to maintain a culture committed to its values and not just to its bottom line.

APPLICATION

Maintain Your Culture

Q: Can you articulate what your company culture is?

Q: If you asked the same question of your employees, would their answer be the same as yours?

Q: What can you do to reinforce the key (positive) elements of your company culture?

For more resources, go to TheBezosLetters.com

Chapter Twelve

Principle 12: Focus on High Standards

"Building **a culture of high standards is well worth the effort**, and there are many benefits. Naturally and most obviously, you're going to build better products and services for customers—this would be reason enough! Perhaps a little less obvious: people are drawn to high standards—they help with recruiting and retention. More subtle: a culture of high standards is protective of all the 'invisible' but crucial work that goes on in every company. I'm talking about the work that no one sees. The work that gets done when no one is watching. In a high standards culture, doing that work well is its own reward—it's part of what it means to be a professional." —Bezos (2017 Letter)

There's an old saying in business: "If you think it's expensive to hire a professional, wait until you hire an amateur."

It's been attributed to a number of people, but the point is true. When scaling a company, investing in high standards is not a luxury, it is a *must*. High standards are an investment you need for your business to scale. Consider the following situations:

- Need ten people to assemble products? It will only happen as fast as the slowest contributor.
- Does attention to detail matter in your organization? You will be dragged down having to correct mistakes made by your least attentive team member.
- Do you want to deliver quality products? If products aren't what people expect, the negative reviews can be devastating.

Investing in high standards with your people and products allows you to move fast and scale big. Fast and accurate workers allow you to sell more products. Attentive employees reduce the resources you need to dedicate to correcting mistakes. And quality components reduce returns, negative reviews, and customer service demands.

For those reasons, if you want to do business with Amazon, expect to be held to tremendously high standards. Two famous examples of Amazon's high standards include getting a job at Amazon and third parties doing business with Amazon.

"Bar Raisers" and Amazon Job Applicants

If you have the opportunity to interview for a position at Amazon, expect the process to focus as much on high standards as it does on your work history or educational background. And expect to encounter people you may not be accustomed to meeting in an interview, including people Amazon refers to as "Bar Raisers."

Bar Raisers are a group of hand-picked people within the company who have demonstrated success at hiring people with very high standards and who have received specialized training.

During the interview process (this is especially true with executive positions) there is usually at least one Bar Raiser present. Bar Raisers have veto power that no one can override—including Bezos or the hiring manager. Nobody who is hired for a position utilizing a Bar Raiser can get hired without the Bar Raiser's "blessing."

Again, in the very first Shareholder Letter from 1997, Bezos made it clear:

> "It's not easy to work here (when I interview people I tell them, 'You can work long, hard, or smart, but at Amazon.com you can't choose two out of three'), but we are working to build something important, something that matters to our customers, something that we can all tell our grandchildren about. Such things aren't meant to be easy. We are incredibly fortunate to have this group of dedicated employees whose sacrifices and passion build Amazon.com." —Bezos (1997 Letter)

But Bar Raisers are not the only way Amazon invests in high standards for applicants at Amazon. Another way Amazon supports high standards is through the three questions all interviewers are asked to consider before making their final decision. From the 1998 Shareholder Letter:

> "Work Hard, Have Fun, Make History

> "It would be impossible to produce results in an environment as dynamic as the Internet without extraordinary people. Working to create a little bit of history isn't supposed to be easy, and, well, we're finding that things are as they're supposed to be! We now have a team of 2,100 smart, hard-

working, passionate folks who put customers first. Setting the bar high in our approach to hiring has been, and will continue to be, the single most important element of Amazon.com's success.

"During our hiring meetings, we ask people to consider three questions before making a decision:

"*Will you admire this person?* If you think about the people you've admired in your life, they are probably people you've been able to learn from or take an example from. For myself, I've always tried hard to work only with people I admire, and I encourage folks here to be just as demanding. Life is definitely too short to do otherwise.

"*Will this person raise the average level of effectiveness of the group they're entering?* We want to fight entropy. The bar has to continuously go up. I ask people to visualize the company 5 years from now. At that point, each of us should look around and say, 'The standards are so high now—boy, I'm glad I got in when I did!'

"*Along what dimension might this person be a superstar?* Many people have unique skills, interests, and perspectives that enrich the work environment for all of us. It's often something that's not even related to their jobs. One person here is a National Spelling Bee champion (1978, I believe). I suspect it doesn't help her in her everyday work, but it does make working here more fun if you can occasionally snag her in the hall with a quick challenge: 'onomatopoeia'!" —Bezos (1998 Letter)

Many people can sense someone they *don't* admire; sometimes that's referred to as a gut feeling that the person will not be a good fit. But how many people consider that question so intentionally?

And what about the second question, whether the person will raise the average level of effectiveness of the group they're entering? That question forces you to not hire a below-average employee. Otherwise, they wouldn't raise the average level of effectiveness.

And could they be a superstar? Looking for dimensions in which the person would be considered a superstar forces an interviewer to look for specific traits for high achievement. Identifying those superstar traits also helps the team best position the new employee to succeed.

Bar Raisers and questions such as these help Amazon continuously raise the bar for every new employee and create a system only A-Players make it through. This is important because true A-Players not only perform well but they also want to be surrounded by other A-Players. They are not threatened by other high-performers; they want to work with other high-performers because it helps the group achieve bigger and better things. A-Players get extremely frustrated with B-Players or C-Players slowing things down or making mistakes.

B-Players, on the other hand, are generally afraid of A-Players, because A-Players can make their performance look poor. That is why B-players usually hire C-players, and below.

To maintain high standards as an organization, you have to be ruthless about the people you hire. Or it will have a cascading effect… you lower the bar, then the person you hire lowers the bar, etc. The spiral will continue downward until you're left with a mediocre company that no longer maintains high standards.

Amazon is known as a demanding work environment. It is a place that can challenge the best employees. It can sometimes even be too demanding for A-Players.

But teams of A-Players make demanding environments *less* demanding; each A-Player can focus on their tasks and rely on the support they will receive from other A-Players doing their jobs well.

High standards will always be the core of the company, at least as long as Bezos is in charge.

> *"Amazon Leadership Principle*—Insist on the Highest Standards: Leaders have relentlessly high standards—many people may think these standards are unreasonably high. Leaders are continually raising the bar and drive their teams to deliver high-quality products, services, and processes. Leaders ensure that defects don't get sent down the line and that problems are fixed so they stay fixed."

Amazon.com has information on how to conduct an interview with Amazon.[35] From the website it says:

> "Our interviews are rooted in behavioral-based questions which ask about past situations or challenges you've faced and how you handled them, using Leadership Principles to guide the discussion. We avoid brain teasers (e.g., 'How many windows are in Manhattan?') as part of the interview process. We've researched this approach and have found that those types of questions are unreliable when it comes to predicting a candidate's success at Amazon.

> "Here are some examples of behavioral-based questions:

> - Tell me about a time when you were faced with a problem that had a number of possible solutions. What was the problem and how did you determine the course of action? What was the outcome of that choice?
> - When did you take a risk, make a mistake, or fail? How did you respond, and how did you grow from that experience?
> - Describe a time you took the lead on a project.

- What did you do when you needed to motivate a group of individuals or promote collaboration on a particular project?
- How have you leveraged data to develop a strategy?

"Keep in mind, Amazon is a data-driven company. When you answer questions, your focus should be on the question asked, ensure your answer is well-structured and provide examples using metrics or data if applicable. Reference recent situations whenever possible."

Suffice it to say, in order to have high standards, you need to know what your standards are. Amazon is very clear that they know their standards. Amazon didn't start out with a full list of Leadership Principles, they started with just a few and built on them as Amazon grew. Before you can interview candidates to see if they are a good fit for your company, you have to have a benchmark for comparison and know what variables you are measuring.

Open-ended questions, like the ones Amazon has learned to ask, are extremely valuable but can be unhelpful, and even difficult, if you don't know what you're looking for. It's not about just asking open-ended, provocative questions. It's about finding out if someone is going to fit in and rise to the top of your business or organization.

Investing in Maintaining High Standards for Third Parties

In the summer of 2018, Amazon announced a program offering entrepreneurs a chance to earn up to $300,000 a year by starting their own business making Amazon deliveries. For as little as a $10,000 initial investment, people could start a business as an Amazon driver. Amazon would provide access to the best price for delivery vans and insurance. It would also provide a steady stream of packages for them to deliver and specific routes they can get used to.[36]

So, what's the catch?

Not everyone will be able to maintain the high standards Amazon demands of third parties. While the financial rewards of the business model are enticing for delivery drivers, Amazon makes it clear that this opportunity will require hard work.

Consider the four things Amazon lists as needs for candidates.

First, it requires "Customer obsession: You start with the customer and work backwards." (Sound familiar?)

Second, it requires good leadership skills: "Leadership: You love people! You are great at leading and retaining a team of drivers." In other words, Amazon is looking for people who want to grow, not drivers who want a job.

Third, drivers must "Deliver results: Your can-do attitude inspires your team to handle labor-intensive delivery work, even when challenges arise." This will be hard work, labor-intensive, and challenging.

Finally, each person must have "Resilience: You're capable of dealing with the ambiguity of a fast-paced, ever-changing business." Many people crumble with ambiguity, fast pace, and an ever-changing business. If that's you, Amazon doesn't want you to apply.

Contrast that with what Uber and Lyft promote to potential drivers. Uber, for example, promotes flexibility and getting paid fast.[37] Lyft promotes a similar message, noting "The only person you answer to is you. Control where, how, and when you want to earn—whether that's on your way to the office, while your daughter's at school, or after night classes."[38]

That's far from the customer-obsession, leadership, results, and resilience message Amazon highlights to potential drivers.

A few months after the initial announcement, hundreds of new businesses had been created around the country that employ thousands of drivers delivering packages for Amazon.

High Standards for Non-Amazonians

Amazon has similarly high requirements for third-party sellers using Amazon Marketplace, and the internet is riddled with stories of people getting kicked off the platform for not meeting Amazon's high standards. Take Amazon's description of the standards for example:

"Amazon obsesses over providing our customers the best possible shopping experience. Since the inception of our store, one way we have ensured a great customer experience is by sourcing products directly from Brands and selling them to customers in our store ourselves. In order to preserve that customer experience, we may choose to source products from some Brands for sale by Amazon only. Other Brands can operate as sellers in the Amazon store if they can consistently maintain our standards for customer experience. However, to prevent customer confusion, if any of the Brand's products are sold by Amazon, the Brand may not also sell those products as a seller in the Amazon store.

"We measure customer experience in a number of ways, including high in-stock rates, delivery experience, price competitiveness, and selection coverage. We offer several tools and services to help you meet our standards and sell successfully in the Amazon store, including tools for inventory management and automated pricing, fulfillment services like Fulfillment by Amazon (FBA), and services to grow and protect your Brand like Brand Registry.

"If you cannot maintain our standards for customer experience, you might lose certain privileges associated with operating as a seller in the Amazon store (including having your offers featured on product detail pages), or you might lose the opportunity to operate as a seller in the Amazon store altogether. In that case, you can still offer to sell your products to Amazon so that we can sell them to our customers."[39]

In other words, if you want to sell on Amazon.com you need to maintain the same high standards Amazon expects for its own transactions. If you don't treat a customer with the same respect Amazon demands of its own employees, you run a real risk of having listings removed or getting kicked off the platform completely. You also see that Amazon invests in several tools to help third parties maintain those high standards, such as FBA, a fulfillment service through which Amazon ensures orders are processed to its high standards.

In many ways, Amazon's investment in third-party sellers operates similar to how franchises ensure franchisees maintain brand standards. Pull into any Chick-fil-A location and you can expect to be greeted with a smile, eat the same quality food, and have every "thank you" yield a "my pleasure" in response. When franchisors require franchisees to buy their sauces, burgers, and french fries from a central location, it helps ensure a consistent customer experience. Customers know exactly what to expect when they go to businesses operated as a franchise or similar model. If the experience slips, the corporate headquarters has ways to enforce rules or discipline individual store owners.

Amazon wants the same positive experience to be the case for customers of third-party sellers. When someone shops on Amazon.com, Amazon wants their experience to be consistent and pleasant. And Amazon invests in similar rules and tools to enforce a consistently high customer experience.

How to Invest in High Standards in Your Company

Your company will only be as successful as the standards it maintains.

If your customer experience is inconsistent, you will never be able to scale. If your customer experience is frequently poor, you will never be able to scale. You will only be able to scale when your customer experience is consistently good.

At Amazon, investing in high standards requires a holistic approach. It starts with defining the standards Amazon wants for its customers. It then requires everyone involved in the customer experience to live up to those standards. Finally, it requires investing time and money to consistently improve, such as by asking interviewers whether a candidate will raise the average impact of the group he or she enters.

To invest in high standards in your company, begin by defining the customer experience you want to achieve. Then ask yourself whether the people, products, and services your customers encounter meet those standards. If not, where do you fall short? Do you need to invest in better quality products? Do you need to invest in a more rigorous hiring process? Do you need to require more of your vendors?

You might not have the same influence as Amazon in the marketplace, but any company can consistently improve customer experience. For example, if you are a small business, you might not be able to influence change at a large manufacturer like Amazon can, but you can look for different manufacturers, perhaps a smaller manufacturer who can achieve higher quality and care more about your business.

Creating a culture of high standards allows the business to continue to think like a startup. Once you start deviating from your high standards, you begin the slow, agonizing process of becoming a Day 2 company.

"Day 2 is stasis. Followed by irrelevance. Followed by excruciating, painful decline. Followed by death. And *that* is why it is *always* Day 1."
—Bezos (2016 Letter)

APPLICATION

Focus on High Standards

Q: What are the three or four important characteristics of your highest-performing, highly-successful employees?

Q: Do you (and your hiring managers) focus on those characteristics when hiring?

Q: Who is responsible for "quality control" at your company—and how are they doing?

For more resources, go to TheBezosLetters.com

Chapter Thirteen

Principle 13: Measure What Matters, Question What's Measured, and Trust Your Gut

"Many of the important decisions we make at Amazon.com can be made with data. There is a right answer or wrong answer, a better answer or worse answer, and **math tells us which is which**. These are our favorite kinds of decisions." —Bezos (2005 Letter)

"Math-based decisions command wide agreement, whereas **judgment-based decisions are rightly debated** and often controversial, at least until put into practice and demonstrated. Any institution unwilling to endure controversy must limit itself to decisions of the first type. In our view, doing so would not only limit controversy—it would also significantly limit innovation and long-term value creation." —Bezos (2005 Letter)

"Wandering in business is not efficient ... but it's also not random. It's *guided*—by **hunch, gut, intuition, curiosity**, and powered by a deep conviction that the prize for customers is big enough that it's worth being a little messy and tangential to find our way there."—Bezos (2018 Letter)

Jeff Bezos considers measurements, analytics, and metrics to be a big deal. There are many measurements that stand out, but two of the most important to Bezos are *data* and *money.*

Most businesses know they need to measure and use analytics to understand what's going on in their business. The shift that Bezos makes is that you also need to evaluate *anecdotal* information to make sure you are not letting your data and analytics mislead you. That is, the data you are measuring may be accurate, but if you're measuring the wrong thing, it will not give you the information you need.

Measuring Isn't Only About Financial Data

Data drives everything at Amazon.

Virtually every operational decision is made with data captured within their systems. Over the years Amazon has become very good at tracking customer activity on their website. This is what powers the recommendation engine that tells you "Customer who bought this item also bought..." There are hundreds of thousands of these features powered by algorithms that improve the customer experience.

The Amazon website is constantly being tested to determine the best color, the best button to use, the best placement for reviews, along with thousands of other items. Dubbed "A/B testing," this is a standard way of determining what change will have the most positive impact on consumer experience and behavior. (Simply put, A/B testing, also known as split testing, is an experiment where you divide test subjects into two groups, give one option to one group and another option to the other, and then see which option performs better.)

When you make a small change to a website, you are able to direct a random number of people to the new website and a similar number of people to the existing website and track and monitor the interactions. With this information, you can determine analytically whether visitors liked the change (and shopped more), or the change discouraged shopping and should not be rolled out.

To help manage this process, Amazon created an internal experimentation platform called Weblab. Here is how Bezos explains it:

"We have our own internal experimentation platform called 'Weblab' that we use to evaluate improvements to our websites and products. In 2013, we ran 1,976 Weblabs worldwide, up from 1,092 in 2012, and 546 in 2011. One recent success is our new feature called 'Ask an owner.' It was many years ago that we pioneered the idea of online customer reviews—customers sharing their opinion on a product to help other customers make an informed purchase decision. 'Ask' is in that same tradition. From a product page, customers can ask any question related to the product. *Is the product compatible with my TV/Stereo/PC? Is it easy to assemble? How long does the battery last?* We then route these questions to *owners* of the product. As is the case with reviews, customers are happy to share their knowledge to directly help other customers. Millions of questions have already been asked and answered." —Bezos (2013 Letter)

Every employee at Amazon has access to a common database that provides a massive amount of information about aspects of the operation. One of the ways Amazon encourages invention on behalf of the customer is to reward people for looking at this data and finding new patterns that might indicate that an improvement could benefit the customer experience.

The Amazon Experimentation and Optimization website (the owner of Weblab) describes their mission this way:

"We enable experimentation at massive scale to help Amazon build better products for customers. A/B testing is in Amazon's DNA and we're at the core of how Amazon innovates.

"Amazon's Experimentation & Optimization team builds the core technology powering Amazon's dynamic and growing businesses. We work on the engineering and science that helps leaders at Amazon make rational decisions based on data. We have teams working on causal inference, decision research, experimentation, and forecasting. We build and use practical scientific tools that run on distributed systems used by almost every business and organization at Amazon and its subsidiaries. We help teams at Amazon understand the long-term value their work brings to Amazon, customers, suppliers, partners, and others."[40]

Measuring Financials

When it comes to financial data, most publicly traded companies focus on earnings, earnings per share, and earnings growth rate. But not Bezos.

Bezos prefers *free cash flow* per share.

I'm not a financial analyst; I'm a tech guy and risk expert. I don't run a multibillion-dollar company and, in total transparency, I can't say I totally understand this. But Bezos does. He knows what to measure and what measurements matter.

The term *free cash flow* is the amount of cash flow a company has left over after paying the fixed expenses it needs to keep the doors open—such as rent, necessary equipment, maintenance or upgrades, technology—and keep current in its debt obligations.

Free cash flow is basically the discretionary income, or "spending money," of the corporate world. This is different than the commonly used term "cash flow" because it takes into account the spending a company must make to continue operations on good terms—so it can be a more accurate way to estimate the health of a company from a cash flow perspective.

The 2004 Letter is entirely dedicated to the importance of free cash flow with detailed examples and charts, and Bezos defined what he means by *free cash flow* as it relates to Amazon:

> "Our ultimate financial measure, and the one we most want to drive over the long-term, is free cash flow per share.

> *"Free cash flow* is defined as net cash provided by operating activities less purchases of fixed assets, including capitalized internal-use software and website development, both of which are presented on our statements of cash flows." —Bezos (2004 Letter)

Free cash flow per share is Bezos' and Amazon's preferred way of evaluating its financial health.

Bezos' main point is that typical Wall Street metrics don't always paint an accurate picture of a company's health or value.

That's why the Growth Principle is about measuring what matters.

Bezos dedicated the entire 2004 Letter to Shareowners to free cash flow over earnings per share and continues to use this as part of his financial strategy. Yet every day, millions of investors still focus on earnings, earnings per share, and earnings growth. Is that because those investors reject Bezos' premise? Is it because it's easier to stick to what the mainstream investment market has touted for decades?

No matter what your viewpoint is on free cash flow versus earnings as the best measure of corporate health, Bezos' success running Amazon to maximize free cash flow instead of earnings at least raises the question of whether we are measuring what really matters in our companies.

In a world where a lot of respect is paid to the old saying "What gets measured gets done," this is especially important. Specifically, what will your leadership team ask of their employees if every financial review meeting centers on earnings? Without a doubt they will be focused almost singularly on increasing earnings if you operate under the traditional way of measuring financial progress.

But what if you changed the conversation to free cash flow? They will focus their efforts on improving free cash flow—which is more focused toward long-term thinking.

For your company to measure what matters, you first must identify the ultimate measure of success or progress for *your* organization. If you're looking to grow like Amazon, perhaps free cash flow will be a major focus. Once you make a decision as to your ultimate measure, work with your leaders to identify smaller data points that you can measure to let you know if you are heading in the right direction.

Do this at every level of your business, as a whole organization, with each department, team, position, and with each new project or initiative. At the organizational level, what measures let you know you are heading in the right direction? Keep asking the same measurement questions for each department, team, and position. As you experiment with new initiatives, measure performance consistent with your big goal.

With a clear vision of what matters most, you might end up measuring data points you never thought to be important. And you might end up no longer paying attention to measures you have focused on for years.

But measuring what matters and questioning what's measured helps position you and your team to work together to the most important common goal for your company.

> "Our decisions have consistently reflected this focus. We first measure ourselves in terms of the metrics most indicative of our market leadership: customer and revenue growth, the degree to which our customers continue to purchase from us on a repeat basis, and the strength of our brand." —Bezos (1997 Letter)

Question What You Measure

Amazon has had their fair share of challenges along the way. But when Bezos looks at numbers, he is able to look at the bigger picture as well. At the burst of the internet bubble, Amazon took a big hit with its stock dropping from $113 per share to $6 per share in less than a year.

You may recall, his annual Shareholder Letter that year started with a one-word sentence: "Ouch."

He described that time in an interview with David Rubenstein:

> "That whole period is very interesting, because the stock is not the company, and the company is not the stock. And so, as I watched the stock fall from $113 to $6, I was also watching all of our internal business metrics, number of customers, and profit per unit. You know, everything you can imagine, defects, etc. Every single thing about the business was getting better and fast. As the stock price was going the wrong way, everything inside the company was going the right way.

> "We didn't need to go back to the capital markets. We didn't need more money. The only reason a financial bust, like the internet bubble bursting, is [hard] is it makes it really hard to raise money. But you know, we already had the money we needed. So, we just needed to continue to progress."

He continued,

> "People always accused us of selling dollar bills for 90 cents and said, look, anybody can do that and grow revenues. That's not what we were doing. We always had positive gross margins. It's a fixed-cost business. And so, what I could see from the internal metrics is that at a certain volume level, that we would cover our fixed costs, and the company would be profitable."
> —2018 Interview, *The David Rubenstein Show*, Bloomberg

Trust Your Gut

But Amazon does not blindly use data as the only criteria for making decisions. At the Bush Center's Forum on Leadership at SMU in 2018, Bezos talked about the importance of anecdotes when measuring performance [slightly edited for clarity]:

> "I still have an email address that customers can write to. I see most of those emails. I don't answer very many of them anymore. But I see them, and I forward some of them, the ones that catch my curiosity, I forward them to the executives in charge of that area with a question mark.

> "And that question mark is just a shorthand for, can you look into this? Why is this happening? What's going on?

> "And what I find very interesting because we have tons of metrics, we have weekly business reviews with these metric decks, and we look at so many things about customers. Whether we're delivering on time, whether the packages have too much air in them, and wasteful packaging. And so, we have so many metrics that we monitor.

"The thing I have noticed is that when the anecdotes and the data disagree, the anecdotes are usually right. There's something wrong with the way you're measuring it.

"When you are shipping billions of packages a year, for sure you need good data and metrics. Are you delivering on time? Are you delivering on time in every city? Are you delivering on time to apartment complexes? And are you delivering on time in certain countries? You do need the data.

"But then you need to check that data with your intuition and your instincts. And you need to teach that to all the senior executives and engineering executives."

> "Every anecdote from a customer matters. We research each of them because they tell us something about our processes. It's an audit that is done for us by our customers. We treat them as precious sources of information." —Jeff Wilke, CEO, Worldwide Consumer at Amazon

The bottom line: There will always be tension between data and gut instincts… but you always have to have both.

The Trust of Your Customers

"The reason customers have been receptive in large part to our new initiatives is because we have worked hard to earn their trust with them. Earning trust with customers is a valuable business asset. And if you mistreat their data, they will know it, they will figure it out. Customers are very smart. You should never underestimate customers." —2018

Interview with Mathias Döpfner, CEO, Axel Springer, parent company of
Business Insider[41]

No matter what your position is when it comes to the ultimate
measure of success, whether GAAP accounting or free cashflow per
share, if your customers don't trust you with their data, you're screwed.

Again, data drives everything at Amazon. Virtually every decision
made is made with data that is captured within their systems.

And why is Amazon so focused on data?

The primary reason is to obsess *over* their customers.

APPLICATION

**Measure What Matters, Question What's Measured, and Trust
Your Gut**

Q: Have you identified the key data drivers in your business?

Q: Are you able to sort through all the data you measure and
figure out which metrics really matter?

Q: (You are measuring *something,* right?)

For more resources, go to TheBezosLetters.com

Chapter Fourteen

Principle 14:
Believe It's Always "Day 1"

"As always, I attach a copy of our original 1997 letter. It **remains Day 1**."
—Bezos (2018 Letter)

What does "Day 1" really mean? It's obviously incredibly important to Bezos. He refers back to his 1997 Letter *every year*, reminding shareowners that it will always be Day 1 at Amazon.

But here's what's interesting… Day 1 is a *concept, not a date*.

Amazon was an "online" business. There were no balloons… or streamers… or "Grand Opening" fireworks. The first employee was Bezos himself and then he added programmers, not salespeople.

So why is the idea of Day 1 so important to Jeff Bezos?

185

When I studied the Shareholder Letters along with other documents and interviews of Bezos, two things became clear.

First, Day 1 is representative of all the leadership principles that have helped make Amazon what it is today. It is the anchor for acknowledging and remembering their beginning values and their dogged focus on serving the needs of customers and even "delighting" customers.

Second, Day 1 is a mindset, not a list of steps or strategies. It is the mentality through which all decisions are made. It is designed to keep everyone in the company focused on doing what is *right* in each situation, not just what is *possible* given Amazon's size and influence. Because, like a child's tower of building blocks, if the foundation isn't stable, the tower will come tumbling down. And then it's Day 2. It bears repeating:

> "Day 2 is stasis. Followed by irrelevance. Followed by excruciating, painful decline. Followed by death. And *that* is why it is *always* Day 1."
> —Bezos (2016 Letter)

On Day 1, there are few—if any—things more important than customers.

Like employees living paycheck-to-paycheck, many businesses live customer-to-customer at the beginning. In the early days, some businesses are only one or two customers away from catastrophe.

When Amazon was first launching, Bezos said he knew they were going to make it in the first thirty days. But given the small revenue per customer from book sales, there is no way they could grow without adding customers. They absolutely needed to scale. In fact, they needed to add customers and earn repeat business from each of those customers to become the company they are today.

Thus, from Day 1 on, Amazon has been obsessed with earning business and repeat business. It's obsessed with understanding its customers, what they want, and what they want to avoid. Amazon makes virtually every decision with that in mind.

As Bezos describes it:

> "You can be competitor focused, you can be product focused, you can be technology focused, you can be business model focused, and there are more. But in my view, obsessive customer focus is by far the most protective of Day 1 vitality." —Bezos (2016 Letter)

Resist Proxies

A key part of Amazon's "It's always Day 1" philosophy is what Bezos calls "resisting proxies." In simple terms, proxies (in this context) are any form of excuse people use to blame others for less-than-ideal actions or decisions. They give people an excuse to distance themselves from their actions. Common examples of proxies include policies, procedures, processes, and sometimes even orders from another person.

Have you ever been frustrated by a company representative who couldn't help you with an issue because of "company policy," "procedures don't allow for that," or they were "only following orders"? If so, you have experienced an employee *not* resisting proxies. At Amazon, "company policy" or any other proxy is no excuse for doing the wrong thing for the customer.

Of course, every business needs procedures and processes in place to get things done. They need rules and best practices to operate efficiently. But those policies, procedures, rules, and other proxies should never be used as excuses for not doing the right thing when it comes to serving customers well.

Thus, another way of saying what Bezos describes as "resisting proxies" would be the admonition to "be *okay* with deviating from policies and procedures" when it is the right thing to do for the customer.

Policies and procedures are intended to help guide decisions, but not at the expense of the needs of the customer.

To grow like Amazon and remain a Day 1 company, you must resist letting proxies dictate what your team does. When you get to the point where procedures rigidly dictate everything your team does—without even questioning those procedures—you start to move from Day 1 to Day 2.

Embrace External Trends

Even intelligent and successful companies can have a hard time recognizing how a new trend could up-end their entire business model. In Bezos' words,

> "These big trends are not that hard to spot (they get talked and written about a lot), but they can be strangely hard for large organizations to embrace." —Bezos (2016 Letter)

The biggest impediment to realizing how new trends will impact an organization is the company's attitude toward risk-taking, particularly if the trend is new. Whenever a company becomes entrenched in "doing it the way it's always been done," leadership and the rank-and-file will resist taking risks—and new trends often look risky. In this environment, an employee might believe any type of failure could torpedo their career. For many, it's just not worth it. And thus, begins the process of becoming a Day 2 company.

On Day 1, however, companies are aware of external trends for the very reason that they are new and vulnerable to bigger or more established competitors. So, they look for ways to use trends to grow and serve their customers better. The trick is to keep that Day 1 mindset, even when you've grown into a $100 billion company. What are consumers demanding from other businesses? What are other successful companies starting to do? How can you use that information to serve your customers better?

Speed Trumps Perfection

On Day 1, decisions are made *fast*. Somebody with authority is available to quickly make a decision. Usually that person is the founder. Often, that person is the only person in the company.

On Day 1, you can't wait for perfect and complete information to make a decision. You make the best decision you can with the information you have. But you have to move quickly. As Bezos puts it, a Day 1 culture emphasizes speed over perfection when making decisions. In the context of Day 1, this admonition by Bezos bears repeating:

> "Most decisions should probably be made with somewhere around 70% of the information you wish you had. If you wait for 90%, in most cases, you're probably being slow. Plus, either way, you need to be good at quickly recognizing and correcting bad decisions. If you're good at course correcting, being wrong may be less costly than you think, whereas being slow is going to be expensive for sure." —Bezos (2016 Letter)

This is closely related to one of Amazon's core Leadership Principles, namely to:

> **"Have Backbone; Disagree and Commit:** Leaders are obligated to respectfully challenge decisions when they disagree, even when doing so is uncomfortable or exhausting. Leaders have conviction and are tenacious. They do not compromise for the sake of social cohesion. Once a decision is determined, they commit wholly."

And what about bad decisions? Not a problem.

If you make a Type 2 decision and it turns out to be a bad one, you just quickly make a new decision using the information you gained from your mistake. In other words, a side benefit to the high-velocity decision-making that comes with building a Day 1 culture is the ability and willingness to quickly make another decision when something doesn't go according to plan.

Commit to a Day 1 Culture by Acting and Thinking like a Startup

Bezos' Day 1 mindset can be applied to any type of business in any industry, from startup to large and mature companies. It's not easy to be a Day 1 business, but the key is to remember Day 1 is a *mindset*. Applying Day 1 thinking to a mature company helps you avoid waste and stay focused on what made you successful in the first place.

Working in a startup is draining with long hours and often great sacrifices. But it can also be exhilarating. When a company matures, it is natural for leadership to lose focus on the small (or big) details that helped it grow. Amazon avoids that by using visible and invisible cues and reinforcing the importance of a Day 1 culture in everything they do—from "door desks" to building names, it's all about remembering the key values you started with.

It can be exhausting to maintain the focus and passion you had when your business was truly in Day 1. But I assure you it is much more exhausting to lose your Day 1 thinking, turn the company calendar to Day 2, and see your company fall into the "excruciating, painful decline" that Bezos describes.

To be sure, this kind of decline will happen in slow motion. Months or years of lost focus builds negative momentum. So, the longer you wait, the harder it will be to turn back the calendar to Day 1. No matter what, there will never be a better time than today to start building a Day 1 culture. If you have slipped into Day 2 months or even years ago, you will either slip further into Day 2 or take action to turn back the calendar to Day 1.

In his 2016 Letter, Bezos answered the question,

"Jeff, what does Day 2 look like?"

"I'm interested in the question, how do you fend off Day 2? What are the techniques and tactics? How do you keep the vitality of Day 1, even inside a large organization?

"Such a question can't have a simple answer. There will be many elements, multiple paths, and many traps. I don't know the whole answer, but I may know bits of it. Here's a starter pack of essentials for Day 1 defense: customer obsession, a skeptical view of proxies, the eager adoption of external trends, and high-velocity decision making." —Bezos (2016 Letter)

To put it in other words, your business is either growing or dying. There is no middle ground. And the only way to avoid Day 2 is to... *believe it is always Day 1.*

APPLICATION

Believe It's Always Day 1

Q: If your business is more than five years old, ask yourself: What did we do early on that I wish we were still doing now?

Q: If your business is less than five years old, ask yourself: Ten years from now, even though I hope we're making a lot more money, I hope we haven't stopped doing... what?

Q: No matter how young or old your business is, ask yourself: What can I do regularly to model a "Day 1" mindset?

For more resources, go to TheBezosLetters.com

Chapter Fifteen

A Risk and Growth Mindset

"It is truly Day 1 for the Internet and, if we execute our business plan well, it remains Day 1 for Amazon.com. Given what's happened, it may be difficult to conceive, but we think the **opportunities and risks ahead of us are even greater than those behind us.** We will have to make many conscious and deliberate choices, some of which will be bold and unconventional." —Bezos (1998 Letter)

You probably know the saying, "You've got to play to win."
But Bezos plays to *learn.*
That's the difference between gambling and taking *intentional* risks.

As I said earlier, taking haphazard risks and hoping for a win is like rolling the dice or spinning the wheel—you never know what's going to come up or where the wheel is going to stop.

But with Bezos, he not only takes risks with intentionality, he often takes risks that are *counterintuitive*.

Again, here are some examples:

Amazon Marketplace: The idea of putting a competitor's product on Amazon's sole selling platform seemed outrageous to many. Bezos put competitors on the Amazon site.

Amazon Prime: Shipping was notoriously expensive, and *hardly anyone* paid for shipping for customers (without inflating the price enormously). Bezos offered free shipping with low prices.

Kindle: There were some people who thought electronic books would not be well received by a public that was so used to reading a physical book. Bezos created the Kindle to hold thousands of books and not just be read like a physical book but to be read *better* than a physical book with movable highlights and cross-platform syncing.

Amazon Web Services (AWS): AWS was originally designed to be the internal operating system for just Amazon. Bezos decided to open their proprietary platform to other developers. No one else at the time was providing software as a service and didn't expect this of Amazon (which is what gave them their seven-year lead). Bezos was taking a contrarian approach.

Did Bezos go against the grain? Definitely. Was everything "successful" from the beginning. Of course not.

But Bezos doesn't take reckless risks—reckless risk-taking is a surefire way to go broke fast. He takes risks cautiously and thoughtfully, and it all revolves around how he views success.

Some people may think, "Well sure, Bezos can take risks—he's the richest man in the world." But intentional risk-taking is a mindset... it doesn't matter how much money you have.

When Bezos was driving a Honda Accord and starting out doing an online business when practically *no one* had internet service, he was taking intentional risks and actually investing his money, his parents' money, and his friends' money in those risks. It was a real investment. Yes, it was an investment in a business, but it was also an investment in an idea… the idea of online commerce. And then, like most startups, he had to keep reinvesting in his idea for it to grow and scale.

Bezos doesn't avoid risks at all costs; he invests in risk as a cost of doing business. He actually embraces risk as a way to learn and grow.

As the company took off, it was a huge risk for Bezos to buck Wall Street. They wanted to evaluate the business on quarterly profits, but he used overall company growth (trajectory) as a more accurate picture of how Amazon was doing over the long term.

Today, Bezos is so focused on the long term that he delegates pretty much all of Amazon's day-to-day operations to his team and spends a lot of his time thinking about what Amazon is, what he wants it to be, and what he wants to happen next.

But for Bezos, "next" is happening two or three years into the future. He said recently,

"Friends congratulate me after a quarterly-earnings announcement and say, 'Good job, great quarter,' and I'll say, 'Thank you, but that quarter was baked three years ago.' I'm working on a quarter that'll happen in 2021 right now." —2018 Interview with Randall Lane, *Forbes* magazine[42]

When you're operating in the future, by definition, you are taking intentional risks since you don't know what the future holds.

And now that Amazon has reached the $100 billion mark, here's what Bezos says:

"As a company grows, *everything* needs to scale, including the size of your failed experiments. **If the size of your failures isn't growing, you're not going to be inventing at a size that can actually move the needle.** Amazon will be experimenting at the right scale for a company of our size if we occasionally have multibillion-dollar failures.

"Of course, we won't undertake such experiments cavalierly. We will work hard to make them good bets, but not all good bets will ultimately pay out. This kind of large-scale risk taking is part of the service we as a large company can provide to our customers and to society. The good news for shareowners is that a single big winning bet can more than cover the cost of many losers." —Bezos (2018 Letter)

"Occasionally have multibillion-dollar failures" is hard for even me to grasp.

But, again, that's why Bezos is the master of risk.

How Did Bezos Develop a Risk and Growth Mindset?

Jeff Bezos didn't start out as a bazillionaire. He had a well-paying job that he quit to pursue an online business idea many would have called crazy. He had to ask his parents for around $300,000 to bootstrap his new business idea. Bezos said,

"My dad's first question was, what's the internet? He wasn't making a bet on this company or this concept. He was making a bet on his son." —1998 Lake Forest College Speech[43]

Bezos was frugal, passionate, and willing to take risks to grow his business. He was smart, tenacious, and a zealot when it came to focusing on the customer.

Twenty years later, in 2018, Jeff Bezos was formally designated the wealthiest person in the world by *Forbes* (I think that officially makes him a bazillionaire).

But Jeff Bezos says he "won the lottery" not by becoming the richest man in the world but by having a loving family that's always had his back. He was born to Jackie Gise, a seventeen-year-old high school student, in 1964 in New Mexico and then adopted by his stepfather, Miguel "Mike" Bezos, a petroleum engineer.

From the time he was four years old until he was sixteen, he spent every summer with his maternal grandparents, working at their ranch in south Texas. His grandfather, Lawrence Preston Gise, was an early employee of what became DARPA (Defense Advanced Research Projects Agency). The Department of Defense created this special group within the Pentagon after the Soviet Union launched Sputnik into space. It was made up of its best and brightest scientists and engineers.

But to Jeff Bezos, he was just "Pop."

Bezos spent a lot of time with his grandfather, who he said was:

"...always incredibly respectful of me even when I was little kid. And would entertain long conversations with me about technology and space and anything I was interested in.[44]

"He created the illusion for me when I was four years old that I was helping him on the ranch. Which, of course, cannot have been true. But I believed it."[45]

Bezos said he would ride around in the pickup truck or on a horse and, as he got older, he started to do actual jobs to help around the ranch. He'd help his grandfather fix windmills, build fences, repair heavy machinery, and even perform some veterinary procedures such as sewing up a prolapsed cow. (Which he jokingly says, "some even survived!")

"One of the things that's so interesting about that lifestyle and about my grandfather is he did everything himself. You know, he didn't call a vet if one of the animals was sick; he figured out what to do himself.

"That resourcefulness and 'can do' work ethic was passed down from his grandfather while working the 25,000-acre ranch near Cotulla, Texas."[46]

I can only imagine the conversations Bezos had with his grandfather. I suspect there were many conversations about the (unclassified) work that was being done at DARPA. My guess is these conversations provided additional fuel for Bezos' already active imagination and fascination with the long-term possibilities that space flight offered. Time, hard work, inventing and fixing things, and loving parents and grandparents were a winning combination for a little boy becoming a young man.

Bezos was only five years old when Neil Armstrong stepped on the Moon and seven when the "successful failure" of Apollo 13 took place. It seems reasonable to assume he and his grandfather had long talks about the future of space and what it would mean to go back to the Moon and beyond.

When Bezos was in elementary school, he got some "firsthand" computer experience. In a 2001 interview with the Academy of Achievement, Bezos said,

"There was a company in Houston that had loaned excess mainframe computer time to this little elementary school. And nobody—none of the teachers knew how to operate this computer, nobody did. But there was a stack of manuals and me and a couple of other kids stayed after class and learned how to program this thing."[47]

One of the first things they discovered is that the computer contained a primitive *Star Trek* game, which is what they used the computer for from then on.

The impact of the *Star Trek* TV show and movie franchise can't be underestimated; just ask Alexa for "Earl Grey, hot" (which was said by Captain Jean-Luc Picard on *Star Trek: The Next Generation*) and she will tell you variations of "the replicators on this vessel are not yet operational."

The family moved to Florida where Bezos graduated high school in Miami. He gave the valedictorian speech for his class. His talk was, not surprisingly, about space. His speech idea (he was influenced by Princeton physicist Dr. Gerard O'Neill) was that Earth had limited resources and so he wanted to get manufacturing and humanity off its surface and into space to protect the planet.

Bezos said that Earth should be designated as a National Park that people would visit on vacations from their home in space. It was an intriguing valedictorian speech that even caught the attention of a reporter from the *Miami Herald* who published an article about his talk.[48]

Bezos attended Princeton University with a desire to be a physicist. Bezos tells the story in a *Guardian* article that quantum mechanics ended his physics career. He ended up graduating Princeton with double majors in computer science and electrical engineering. As he explains it,

"One of the great things Princeton taught me is that I'm not smart enough to be a physicist."[49]

He moved to New York City where he met and married his wife and worked in several different jobs in the financial industry and on Wall Street. During this time, he continued to nurture a dream to start his own company.

Here is how he described that time in a speech he gave at Lake Forest College in 1998 when Amazon was only three years old:

"The company was conceived in the spring of 1994. I came across a startling fact in the spring of '94; web usage was growing at 2300% a year. I have to keep in mind that human beings aren't good at understanding exponential growth. It's just not something we see in our everyday life. But things don't grow this fast outside of petri dishes; it just doesn't happen.

"And when I saw this I said, okay, what's a business plan that might make sense in the context of that growth? I made a list of twenty different products that you might be able to sell online. I was looking for the first best product.

"And I chose books, for lots of different reasons. But one primary reason, and that is that there are more items in the book space than there are items in any other category, by far. There are over three million different books worldwide in all languages. The number two product category in that regard is music, with about 300,000 active music CDs.

"And when you have this huge catalog of products, you can build something online that you just can't build any other way. The largest physical bookstores, the largest super stores, (and these are huge stores often converted from bowling alleys and movie theaters) can only carry about 175,000 titles. There are only a few that large.

"In our online catalog, we're able to list over two and a half million different titles and give people access to those titles. And being able to do something online that you can't do in any other way is important.

It's all about the fundamental tenet of building any business, which is creating value proposition for the customer.

"And online, especially three years ago, but even today, and for the next several years, the value proposition that you have to build for customers is incredibly large. And that's because the web is a pain to use today. We've all experienced modem hang-ups and the browsers crash. And there's all sorts of inconveniences, websites are slow, modem speeds are slow.

"So, if you're going to get people to use a website in today's environment, you have to offer them overwhelming compensation for this primitive, infant technology. And I would claim that that compensation has to be so strong, that it's basically the same as saying you can only do things online today that simply can't be done any other way.

"And that's why this huge number of products looked like a winning combination online. There was no other way to have a two-and-a-half-million-title bookstore. You can't do it in a physical store. But you also can't do it in a print catalog. If you were to print the Amazon.com catalog, it would be the size of more than forty New York City phone books."
—1998 Lake Forest College Speech

"He [Bezos] could see that there was this technological tsunami that was arriving. It was going to disintermediate, was going to create new distribution channels, reset economics, change the way we bought and sold. And the question was, which domain shall we apply it to?" —Chris Anderson, Editor-in-Chief, *Wired* magazine

Bezos moved from New York to Seattle for likely two main reasons. That's where Microsoft was headquartered, so there was a pool of exceptional programming talent. There were also two large book distribution centers nearby: Ingram and Baker & Taylor.

He rented a house with a garage, connected to the internet, and in July 1994, Amazon.com was born, setting the stage for Bezos to fulfill his dream of being an entrepreneur.

Faster Horses

You've probably heard the quote attributed to Henry Ford, "If I had asked people what they wanted, they would've told me *faster horses.*"

We all know what happened. Ford didn't make their horses faster; he actually gave them something better—horse*power*—in his automobiles. It wasn't long before no one was driving horses anymore.

Just like the automobile replaced the horse, things are always happening that shift the way we think and do business. There are always new and inventive technologies and products being created that are hidden from our awareness (remember those "skunkworks"?).

The prevailing mindset at the time was "faster horses." Ford had the idea to design and test something new (an affordable automobile), build it (the Model T), accelerate the process (the assembly line), and scale (using local dealerships). There were over fifteen million Model Ts sold by 1927. Ford had a risk and growth mindset.

Which bring us back to the most important element in risk, growth, and success—people.

With their inventive and innovative ideas, these familiar people have had an impact on the world: Henry Ford, Thomas Edison, Steve Jobs, and J.K. Rowling are just a few. Of course, there are many more I could have added.

But here's the point: Using the same risk and growth mindset that Bezos and these others have used, I believe we can all change the world (wherever we are) and make our mark for the better.

And that's really what a risk and growth mindset is all about.

Chapter Sixteen

Beyond Amazon

"Space: the final frontier. These are the voyages of the starship *Enterprise*. Its continuing mission: to explore strange new worlds, to seek out new life and new civilizations, to boldly go where no one has gone before." —*Star Trek*

As big as Amazon is, to Bezos, Amazon is merely the means to an even *bigger* end. Six or seven generations from now, when his future great-grandchildren have great-grandchildren, Jeff Bezos wants there to be a dynamic, growing civilization being freely enjoyed in space… and he's using his business, Amazon, to fund that dream.

In 2000, just a few years after Amazon had started, Jeff Bezos quietly created a little company called Blue Origin (blue for the earth and origin for where we now live in the universe). Today, Blue Origin is on the forefront of private space exploration. On the Blue Origin website, he narrates:

> "Ever since I was five years old—that's when Neil Armstrong stepped onto the surface of the Moon—I've been passionate about space, rockets, rocket engines, space travel.

> "I think we all have passions, and you don't get to choose them; they pick you, but you have to be alert to them. You have to be looking for them.

> "This is the most important work I'm doing.

> "It's a simple argument: this is the best planet. And so, we face a choice. As we move forward, we're going to have to decide whether we want a civilization of stasis; we will have to cap population, we will have to cap energy usage per capita, or we can fix that problem by moving out into space.

> "The problem, of course, is space travel; it's just so expensive. And so, we need to figure out how to lower the cost, and the incredible opportunity is reusability. And so, what we really need is operational, realistic, practical, pragmatic reusability just like you see with commercial aviation. That's the key. If we can do that it will dramatically lower the cost of getting people into space.

> "I wish that there could be a bunch of very entrepreneurial startup companies doing amazing things in space.

> "The idea of going to the Moon was so impossible that people actually used it as a metaphor for impossibilities. What I would hope to take away from that is that anything you set your mind to, you can do.

"[Wernher] Von Braun said, after the lunar landing, 'I've learned to use the word impossible with great caution,' and I hope you guys take that attitude about your lives."[50]

As competitive as Bezos may seem, I don't believe his ventures into space are about winning a "competition," like with Elon Musk or Sir Richard Branson.

I actually believe he is building the scaffolding, or infrastructure, to make future life in space possible. He recognizes that the scaffolding for Amazon had been built before he even came up with the idea for an online business:

"If I look at what Amazon was able to do twenty years ago, we didn't have to build a transportation network, it already existed. That heavy lifting was in place. We didn't have to build a payment system; that heavy lifting had already been done. It was the credit card system. We didn't have to build and put a computer on every desk. That had already been done too, mostly for playing games by the way, and so on. All the pieces of heavy lifting were already in place twenty years ago, and that's why, with a million dollars, I could start this company.

"There are even better examples on the internet over the last twenty years. Facebook started in a dorm room. I guarantee you two kids cannot build a giant space company in their dorm rooms. It's impossible but I want to create the heavy lifting infrastructure. Do the hard part [now] so that a future generation of kids in the dorm room will be able to create a giant space company." —2018 Forum on Leadership, "Closing Conversation with Jeff Bezos"

How Bezos Identified the Invaluable Role of Infrastructure

It's almost hard to imagine a world without the internet and instantaneous connectivity. Amazon was able to harness that connectivity by using the "scaffolding" of existing services. For example, would Prime two-day shipping have been possible without FedEx leading the way in 1973 "when it absolutely, positively needs to be there overnight"? Or would online shopping from anywhere have happened without the iPhone that came out in 2007?

Bezos has always recognized that there was a foundational infrastructure in place for Amazon to happen.

"Today we deliver 5 billion-plus units a year, we have $100 billion in sales, hundreds of thousands of employees, and we're not alone. If you look at the Internet, that's a big industry now, made up of a bunch of very healthy, entrepreneurial, thriving companies of all shapes and sizes, pursuing different missions. It's very dynamic and very exciting. That happened very fast ... just two decades to see that kind of dynamism unfold.

"I can tell you why it happened. If you think about e-commerce, all of the heavy lifting was already done. We had all these big pieces of infrastructure in place. For Amazon to be an e-commerce company in 1995, we didn't have to roll out a national transportation network to deliver parcel packages. The Postal Service was already there. UPS was already there. That would have been billions of dollars in assets and taken many decades to deploy, but it was already there. It wasn't there for e-commerce; it was there for other reasons.

"Same thing, the Internet, we had a phone network. You remember these little modems that we could attach, those acoustic modems, and we could do Internet in early days standing on top of another huge piece of infrastructure, which was the local and long-distance telephone network. It wasn't designed for the Internet. It wasn't designed for e-commerce. It was designed for voice calls, but it was there. Same thing with remote payments: You had credit cards and so on. So, there were a bunch of pieces already existing.

"If you want to see a dynamic golden age with entrepreneurial energy where thousands of entrepreneurs could be doing amazing things in space, we can't do that. We haven't seen that in 50 years, and the reason we haven't seen it is because the big heavy lifting pieces are not yet in place. There may be multiple things that would have to happen before you can see that kind of gigantic leap, but I don't think so. I really think it's just one big piece, and it's that we need much lower-cost access to space."[51]

The idea behind creating infrastructure is like the quote, "standing on the shoulders of giants." Meaning, what's happened today is because of the extraordinary efforts of others in the past.

Bezos is working today to create a "past" for those in the future to use.

***

Blue Origin has as its motto the Latin phrase *Gradatim Ferociter* (Step by Step, Ferociously).

"We are not in a race, and there will be many players in this human endeavor to go to space to benefit Earth. Blue's part in this journey is building a road to space with our reusable launch vehicles, so our children can build the future. We will go about this step by step because it is an illusion that skipping steps gets us there faster. Slow is smooth, and smooth is fast."[52]

Because Bezos is "building a road to the future," I believe he is using the same Growth Cycles and 14 Growth Principles at Blue Origin that he used building Amazon in order to make his dream of private space travel possible. He is Testing, Building, Accelerating, and Scaling. I have taken the 14 Growth Principles and loosely applied them to Blue Origin here:

The Anderson 14 Growth Principles (loosely applied to Blue Origin)

Test

1. **Encourage "Successful Failure"**—Blue Origin begins by experimenting small to see what works best (space exploration is a bit pricey, even for Bezos).
2. **Bet on Big Ideas**—Space travel is, obviously, a big idea.
3. **Practice Dynamic Invention and Innovation**—They have to invent and create for the unknowns in space travel.

Build

4. **Obsess Over Customers**—Their customers are future passengers, third parties, and our great-great-great-grandchildren.
5. **Apply Long-Term Thinking**—They're creating new ways for life to be lived hundreds of years from now.
6. **Understand Your Flywheel**—Blue Origin started in 2000 and they have gained momentum as they have learned, grown, and expanded their business to create reusable vehicles for space travel.

Accelerate

7. **Generate High-Velocity Decisions**—Decisions are made as fast as possible but also made with prudence at the same time.

The mascot for Blue Origin is the tortoise because risky (life and death) decisions have to be like the tortoise in *The Tortoise and the Hare*: "slow is smooth, and smooth is fast."

8. **Make Complexity Simple**—Blue Origin is working to take the average person, not just astronauts, into space.

9. **Accelerate Time with Technology**—Technological advancement is being created and developed to make space travel common and fast.

10. **Promote Ownership**—Space travel is privately owned and not waiting for government programs.

Scale

11. **Maintain Your Culture**—A culture focused on space exploration is, by definition, one where there is a common goal to achieve.

12. **Focus on High Standards**—Only the best and the brightest will get us safely into space.

13. **Measure What Matters, Question What's Measured, and Trust Your Gut**—Everything must be measured, tested, quantified, and replicated to assure safety, but when your instincts contradict the data, ask again, and test again.

14. **Believe It's Always Day 1**—It really is always Day 1 at Blue Origin. Belief is a mindset that's crucial for getting into space.

What is the Biggest Risk?

Amazon, the business, is fueling Jeff Bezos' even bigger dream and passion. Amazon may be, in fact, his personal flywheel. Amazon is the hard push that gets space exploration going, and as it takes off, it *will* gain momentum.

What this tells me is the *Growth Cycles* and *The Anderson 14 Growth Principles* have been essential to growing Amazon, and de facto, Blue Origin, and can be applied to virtually any business, any organization, anywhere.

I'm convinced Jeff Bezos' willingness and mindset to take calculated risks to build and grow Amazon is a result of his fascination with space, his time spent helping his grandfather on the ranch, and an inventive mind that developed from an early age.

When you follow these Growth Cycles and 14 Growth Principles you, too, can grow your business like Amazon.

Yes, sending people to space is risky. Business growth is risky. Life is risky.

But here's the question: What if the biggest risk is actually not taking *enough* risk?

***

At the end of the *Apollo 13* movie, Commander Jim Lovell said:

"I sometimes catch myself looking up at the Moon, remembering the changes of fortune in our long voyage, thinking of the thousands of people who worked to bring the three of us home.

"I look up at the Moon and wonder, when will we be going back, and who will that be?"

2018 Letter to Shareowners with The Anderson Growth Principles (highlighted)

To our shareowners:

Something strange and remarkable has happened over the last 20 years. Take a look at these numbers:

1999	3%
2000	3%
2001	6%
2002	17%
2003	22%
2004	25%
2005	28%
2006	28%
2007	29%
2008	30%
2009	31%
2010	34%
2011	38%
2012	42%
2013	46%

2014	49%
2015	51%
2016	54%
2017	56%
2018	58%

The percentages represent the share of physical gross merchandise sales sold on Amazon by independent third-party sellers—mostly small- and medium-sized businesses—as opposed to Amazon retail's own first party sales. Third-party sales have grown from 3% of the total to 58%. To put it bluntly:

Third-party sellers are kicking our first party butt. Badly.

And it's a high bar too because our first-party business has grown dramatically over that period, from $1.6 billion in 1999 to $117 billion this past year. The compound annual growth rate for our first-party business in that time period is 25%. But in that same time, third-party sales have grown from $0.1 billion to $160 billion—a compound annual growth rate of 52%. To provide an external benchmark, eBay's gross merchandise sales in that period have grown at a compound rate of 20%, from $2.8 billion to $95 billion.

Why did independent sellers do so much better selling on Amazon than they did on eBay? And why were independent sellers able to grow so much faster than Amazon's own highly organized first-party sales organization? There isn't one answer, but we do know one extremely important part of the answer:

We helped independent sellers compete against our first-party business by investing in and offering them *the very best-selling tools we could imagine and build* (*12 Focus on High Standards*). There are many such tools, including tools that help sellers manage inventory, process payments, track shipments, create reports, and sell across borders—and we're inventing more every year. But of great importance are Fulfillment by Amazon and the Prime membership program. In combination, these two programs **meaningfully improved the customer experience** (*4 Obsess Over Customers*) of buying from independent sellers. With the success of these two programs now so well established, it's difficult for most people to fully appreciate today just how radical those two offerings were at the time we launched them. **We invested in both of these programs at significant financial risk and after much internal debate** (*2 Bet on Big Ideas*). We had to continue investing significantly over time as we experimented with different ideas and iterations. We could not foresee with certainty what those programs would eventually look like, let alone whether they would succeed, but they were pushed forward with intuition and heart, and nourished with optimism.

Intuition, curiosity, and the power of wandering

From very early on in Amazon's life, we knew we wanted to **create a culture** (*11 Maintain Your Culture*) of builders—people who are curious, explorers. They like to invent. Even when they're experts, they are "fresh" with a beginner's mind. They see the way we do things as just the way we do things now. A builder's mentality helps us approach big, hard-to-solve opportunities with a humble conviction that success can come through iteration: invent, launch, reinvent, relaunch, start over, rinse, repeat, again and again. They know **the path to success is anything but straight** (*1 Successful Failure*).

Sometimes (often actually) in business, **you *do* know where you're going, and when you do, you can be efficient** (*6 Understand Your*

Flywheel). Put in place a plan and execute. In contrast, wandering in business is not efficient ... but it's also not random. It's *guided*—by hunch, gut, intuition, curiosity, and powered by a deep conviction that the prize for customers is big enough that it's worth being a little messy and tangential to find our way there. Wandering is an essential counter-balance to efficiency. You need to employ both. The outsized discoveries—the "non-linear" ones—are highly likely to require wandering.

AWS's millions of customers range from startups to large enterprises, government entities to nonprofits, each looking to build better solutions for their end users. We spend a lot of time thinking about what those organizations want and what the people inside them—developers, dev managers, ops managers, CIOs, chief digital officers, chief information security officers, etc.—want.

Much of what we build at AWS is based on *listening* to customers. It's critical to ask customers what they want, listen carefully to their answers, and figure out a plan to provide it thoughtfully and quickly (**speed matters in business!)** *(7 Generate High-Velocity Decisions).* No business could thrive without that kind of customer obsession. But it's also not enough. The biggest needle movers will be things that customers don't know to ask for. We must invent on their behalf. We have to tap into our own inner imagination about what's possible.

AWS itself—as a whole—is an example. No one asked for AWS. No one. Turns out the world was in fact ready and hungry for an offering like AWS but didn't know it. **We had a hunch** *(3 Practice Dynamic Invention and Innovation),* followed our curiosity, took the necessary financial risks, and began building—reworking, experimenting, and iterating countless times as we proceeded.

Within AWS, that same pattern has recurred many times. For example, we invented DynamoDB, a highly scalable, low latency key-value database now used by thousands of AWS customers. And on the listening-carefully-to-customers side, we heard loudly that companies felt constrained by their commercial database options and had been unhappy with their database providers for decades—these offerings are expensive, proprietary, have high-lock-in and punitive licensing terms. We spent several years building our own database engine, Amazon Aurora, a fully-managed MySQL and PostgreSQL-compatible service with the same or better durability and availability as the commercial engines, but at one-tenth of the cost. We were *not* surprised when this worked.

But we're also optimistic about specialized databases for specialized workloads. Over the past 20 to 30 years, companies ran most of their workloads using relational databases. The broad familiarity with relational databases among developers made this technology the go-to even when it wasn't ideal. Though sub-optimal, the data set sizes were often small enough and the acceptable query latencies long enough that you could make it work. But today, many applications are storing very large amounts of data—terabytes and petabytes. And the requirements for apps have changed. Modern applications are driving the need for low latencies, real-time processing, and the ability to process millions of requests per second. It's not just key-value stores like DynamoDB, but also in-memory databases like Amazon ElastiCache, time series databases like Amazon Timestream, and ledger solutions like Amazon Quantum Ledger Database—the right tool for the right job saves money and **gets your product to market faster** *(9 Accelerate Time with Technology)*.

We're also plunging into helping companies harness Machine Learning. We've been **working on this for a long time** (5 Apply Long-Term Thinking), and, as with other important advances, our initial attempts to externalize some of our early internal Machine Learning tools were failures. It took years of wandering—experimentation, iteration, and refinement, as well as valuable insights from our customers—to enable us to find SageMaker, which launched just 18 months ago. SageMaker removes the heavy lifting, complexity, and guesswork from each step of the machine learning process—democratizing AI. Today, thousands of customers are building machine learning models on top of AWS with SageMaker. We continue to enhance the service, including by adding new reinforcement learning capabilities. Reinforcement learning has a steep learning curve and many moving parts, which has largely put it out of reach of all but the most well-funded and technical organizations, until now. None of this would be possible without a culture of curiosity and a willingness to try totally new things on behalf of customers. And customers are responding to our customer-centric wandering and listening—AWS is now a $30 billion annual run rate business and growing fast.

Imagining the impossible

Amazon today remains a small player in global retail. We represent a low single-digit percentage of the retail market, and there are much larger retailers in every country where we operate. And that's largely because nearly 90% of retail remains offline, in brick and mortar stores. For many years, we considered how we might serve customers in physical stores, but felt we needed first to invent something that would really delight customers in that environment. With Amazon Go, we had a clear vision. Get rid of the worst thing about physical retail: checkout lines. No one likes to wait in line. Instead, we imagined a store where you could walk in, pick up what you wanted, and leave.

Getting there was hard. Technically hard. It required the efforts of hundreds of smart, dedicated computer scientists and engineers around the world. We had to design and build our own proprietary cameras and shelves and invent new computer vision algorithms, including the ability to stitch together imagery from hundreds of cooperating cameras. And we had to do it in a way where the technology worked so well that **it simply receded into the background, invisible** (8 Make Complexity Simple). The reward has been the response from customers, who've described the experience of shopping at Amazon Go as "magical." We now have 10 stores in Chicago, San Francisco, and Seattle, and are excited about the future.

Failure needs to scale too

As a company grows, everything needs to scale, including the size of your failed experiments. If the size of your failures isn't growing, you're not going to be inventing at a size that can actually move the needle. Amazon will be experimenting at the right scale for a company of our size if we occasionally have multibillion-dollar failures. Of course, we won't undertake such experiments cavalierly. We will work hard to make them good bets, but not all good bets will ultimately pay out. This kind of large-scale risk taking is part of the service we as a large company can provide to our customers and to society. The good news for shareowners is that a single big winning bet can more than cover the cost of many losers.

Development of the Fire phone and Echo was started around the same time. While the Fire phone was a failure, we were able to take our learnings (as well as the developers) and accelerate our efforts building

Echo and Alexa. The vision for Echo and Alexa was inspired by the Star Trek computer. The idea also had origins in two other arenas where we'd been building and wandering for years: machine learning and the cloud. From Amazon's early days, machine learning was an essential part of our product recommendations, and AWS gave us a front row seat to the capabilities of the cloud. After many years of development, Echo debuted in 2014, powered by Alexa, who lives in the AWS cloud.

No customer was asking for Echo. This was definitely us wandering. Market research doesn't help. If you had gone to a customer in 2013 and said, "Would you like a black, always-on cylinder in your kitchen about the size of a Pringles can that you can talk to and ask questions, that also turns on your lights and plays music?" I guarantee you they'd have looked at you strangely and said "No, thank you."

Since that first-generation Echo, customers have purchased more than 100 million Alexa-enabled devices. Last year, we improved Alexa's ability to understand requests and answer questions by more than 20%, while adding billions of facts to make Alexa more knowledgeable than ever. Developers doubled the number of Alexa skills to over 80,000, and customers spoke to Alexa tens of billions more times in 2018 compared to 2017. The number of devices with Alexa built-in more than doubled in 2018. There are now more than 150 different products available with Alexa built-in, from headphones and PCs to cars and smart home devices. Much more to come!

One last thing before closing. As I said in the first shareholder letter more than 20 years ago, our focus is on hiring and retaining versatile and talented employees who can **think like owners** (10 Promote Ownership). Achieving that requires investing in our employees, and, as with so many other things at Amazon, we use **not just analysis but also intuition** (13

Measure What Matters, Question What's Measured, and Trust Your Gut) and heart to find our way forward.

Last year, we raised our minimum wage to $15-an-hour for all full-time, part-time, temporary, and seasonal employees across the U.S. This wage hike benefitted more than 250,000 Amazon employees, as well as over 100,000 seasonal employees who worked at Amazon sites across the country last holiday. We strongly believe that this will benefit our business as we invest in our employees. But that is not what drove the decision. We had always offered competitive wages. But we decided it was time to lead—to offer wages that went beyond competitive. We did it because it seemed like the right thing to do.

Today I challenge our top retail competitors (you know who you are!) to match our employee benefits and our $15 minimum wage. Do it! Better yet, go to $16 and throw the gauntlet back at us. It's a kind of competition that will benefit everyone.

Many of the other programs we have introduced for our employees came as much from the heart as the head. I've mentioned before the Career Choice program, which pays up to 95% of tuition and fees towards a certificate or diploma in qualified fields of study, leading to in-demand careers for our associates, even if those careers take them away from Amazon. More than 16,000 employees have now taken advantage of the program, which continues to grow. Similarly, our Career Skills program trains hourly associates in critical job skills like resume writing, how to communicate effectively, and computer basics. In October of last year, in continuation of these commitments, we signed the President's Pledge to America's Workers and announced we will be upskilling 50,000 U.S. employees through our range of innovative training programs.

Our investments are not limited to our current employees or even to the present. To train tomorrow's workforce, we have pledged $50 million, including through our recently announced Amazon Future Engineer program, to support STEM and CS education around the country for elementary, high school, and university students, with a particular focus on attracting more girls and minorities to these professions. We also continue to take advantage of the incredible talents of our veterans. We are well on our way to meeting our pledge to hire 25,000 veterans and military spouses by 2021. And through the Amazon Technical Veterans Apprenticeship program, we are providing veterans on-the-job training in fields like cloud computing.

A huge thank you to our customers for allowing us to serve you while always challenging us to do even better, to our shareowners for your continuing support, and to all our employees worldwide for your hard work and pioneering spirit. Teams all across Amazon are *listening* to customers and *wandering* on their behalf!

As always, I attach a copy of our original 1997 letter. **It remains Day 1** *(14 Believe It's Always Day 1).*

Sincerely,

/s/ JEFFREY P. BEZOS
Jeffrey P. Bezos
Founder and Chief Executive Officer
Amazon.com, Inc.

Amazon Commonly Used Terms

1-Click Shopping®: A shopping method patented by Amazon in 1998 that allows customers to pay with payment details stored on Amazon's servers. Thus, Amazon customers can make a purchase with a single mouse click. Amazon received a patent on the process in 1999.

Amazon as The World's Most Customer-Centric Company: Bezos repeatedly uses this phrase, emphasizing that Amazon keeps the customer as a focal point. Taken from their SEC 10-K filing.

Amazon Fresh: Service for grocery items (and some 500,000 other items of different categories) trialed in Seattle for five years, then rolled out to other cities as well.

Amazon Lockers: Amazon Lockers are secure, self-service kiosks where you can pick up Amazon.com packages at a time and place that is convenient for you.

Amazon Marketplace: In 2001, this platform allowed third-party sellers to display their products on the same page as Amazon products, allowing them direct access to Amazon customers. The fee to Amazon to participate is an average of 15 percent.

Amazon Web Services (AWS): Amazon Web Services (AWS) is a secure cloud service platform, offering computer power, database storage, content delivery, and other functionality to help businesses scale and grow.

American Customer Satisfaction Index: Also known as ACSI, it measures customer satisfaction in a wide range of products and services across the United States. It is also considered to be an economic indicator. It was launched in 1994 by researchers with the National Quality Research Center at the University of Michigan.

Amazon Auctions: One of Amazon's major 1999 initiatives. Reportedly launched to compete with eBay. It failed and led to zShops, which would later become Marketplace.

AWS: See Amazon Web Services.

Capital Efficient Business Model: Discussed in the 1999 Letter, Amazon had annualized sales of $2 billion, which only required less than $600 million in inventory and fixed assets, only using $62 million in operating cash cumulatively in previous years. This cycle benefits the company as it continues to grow.

Career Choice: Amazon pays for 95 percent of the tuition of Amazon employees taking courses for in-demand fields.

Chaotic Storage: Inventory items are stored on shelves anywhere there's an empty space. This means any storage bin could have five completely different items stored next to each other. It's estimated that Amazon can store 25 percent more inventory in the same space than traditional warehouses, using technology to more than make up for the perceived inefficiency.

Contacts Per Order: One of Amazon's most important measures of customer satisfaction, counting how many contacts are made per client, per order.

Customer Experience Pillars: Amazon has a firm conviction that customers will consistently want low prices, a vast selection, and fast delivery and that this will not change over time.

Distribution Center: Initially a warehouse and inventory center during Amazon's early days. Its Seattle and Delaware distribution centers were the first ones launched in 1997 and would pioneer its distribution network.

Fulfillment by Amazon (FBA): Amazon has one of the most advanced fulfillment networks in the world. With FBA, vendors can store products in Amazon's fulfillment centers. Amazon picks, packs, ships, and provides customer service for these products. FBA helps businesses scale and reach more customers. Sellers, on average, pay 15 percent for this service.

Fulfillment Center (FC) Network: Vendors ship merchandise to a fulfillment center, and Amazon ships it to customers for them. Inventory management is a prevalent operational problem for many online stores, but it is an essential component of cultivating the best possible customer experience.

Global Selling Program: According to Bezos, the program, which grew over 50 percent in 2017, enables small- and medium-sized businesses to sell products across national borders (for Marketplace sellers who can sell in other countries).

Historical Purchase Data: Part of the equation Amazon uses when making purchase decisions. It looks at how frequently a product was purchased to measure and forecast customer demand.

Information Snacking: In the 2007 Letter, Bezos discusses how humans co-evolve with their tools. New technology has led us to where we consume information in bits and pieces and, he would argue, shorter attention spans.

Instant Order Update: An Amazon.com feature that reminds you that you've already bought a particular item, preventing you from accidentally purchasing the same thing twice.

Leave Share: A company program that allows Amazon employees to share their paid leave with their spouse or domestic partner if their spouse's employer does not provide paid leave.

Look Inside the Book: A service added in 2000 where customers can view high-resolution images of the front and back covers, as well as a reasonable sample of pages of a book they are interested in purchasing.

Personalization: Learning what customers prefer and seeking to improve Amazon.com to cater to these preferences.

Price Elasticity: Bezos points to going against the math by lowering prices even though Amazon can, in fact, raise them. He cited that Amazon has enough data on elasticity such that it has been observed that a reduction in price has resulted in an increase of units sold by a certain percentage.

Ramp Back: Mothers who work at Amazon have additional control over the pace that they ease back into work.

Resist Proxies: According to Bezos, as companies grow, there is a risk of managing proxies, citing processes as an example of a proxy. There is a danger of the proxy becoming the actual thing or product, or what's focused on, and takes the place of a result, instead of a means. Bezos pointed out that the company must own the process and not the other way around.

Search Inside the Book: Users can browse a selection of individual digital pages to help them decide if they want to purchase a book.

Search Suggestions: Added in Amazon's search capability in 2006, where a user can type the first few letters and the search engine will prompt with suggested words or terms.

Self-Service Nature of Platforms: Bezos highlighted that this spurs innovation, as even the most well-meaning gatekeepers can stall progress, especially if they come in the form of seemingly improbable ideas. Fulfillment by Amazon is an example of a self-service platform.

Seller Flex: First launched in India to test how Amazon can adapt its Fulfillment Center network to local logistics and customer needs. Amazon includes in its network parts of local sellers' warehouses, providing operational infrastructure and operating procedures. As of 2015, there are twenty-five functional sites in ten cities.

Service-Oriented Architecture (SOA): Considered the primary building blocks of Amazon technologies, SOA was rolled out in the company long before it became a buzzword. Amazon technologies are implemented as services and allowed to evolve and develop at their own pace.

Skills-Forward: According to Bezos, this entails identifying available skills in an organization and thinking of ways they can be further applied. However, he cautioned that this alone is not a good strategy as existing skills can eventually become outmoded.

Super Saver Shipping: Year-round free shipping on orders over $25 started in 2001.

Transportation Hubs: Amazon considers the available transportation hubs in given locations when deciding where to open a fulfillment center, to arrive at the most efficient, fastest product shipping/deliveries.

Weblab: Amazon's internal experimentation platform used to evaluate products, websites, and other improvements.

Working Backwards: According to Bezos, this entails identifying customer needs and subsequently developing new skills and competencies to meet needs and demands. This would be a strategy paired with a skills-forward approach.

zShops: The succeeding version of Auctions, allowing anyone—from individuals to companies—to set up an online shop.

Acknowledgments

Writing a book is not a solitary endeavor. From the spark of an idea to putting initial thoughts down on paper, to writing a terrible first draft, to delivering a finished manuscript, it takes a wide variety of people to make it all come together. For those of you who have walked with me and helped me along the way, my sincere thanks. I am a blessed man.

I'd like to thank…

My Wife: Karen, you have been my champion for forty-seven years since God first brought us together through Young Life in high school. I'm thankful for your encouragement (okay, and maybe a little bit of nagging!), dedication, love, and belief in me. Thank you doesn't begin to describe my gratitude. I love you, beyond words.

My Daughters and their Husbands: Kelly and Aaron Fish and Stephanie and Dustin Diez, I am so thankful for my girls. You are amazing wives and mothers. It is beautiful to watch your kindness, patience, and willingness to give your all for your family. And my sons-in-law, you love and care for my girls well. And that's the best a father can ask.

My Grandkids: The only thing better than being a Dad is being "Papa" to Connor, Avalyn, Declan, Emma Jane, Brayden, August, and Kinsley Rae.

My Family: My dad was a special man. I am thankful for how he nurtured my love of technology when I was a kid hanging around with him at Burroughs in DC. I think he, and my mom, would have liked this book. Peggy was the best sister ever. She taught me by example that when you put your mind to it, you can accomplish anything you want. I think she, and my brother Dave, would have liked this book, too. I miss them all.

My Downtown Franklin Friends: Thank you for your encouragement and support. I love doing life with all of you: Les and Patsy Clairmont, Ken and Diane Davis, Michael and Gail Hyatt, Dan and Joanne Miller, Ian and Anne Cron, and Chris Elrod.

My Mentors: Jack Shreffler and Bill Cadenhead, thank you for encouraging me to research and test.

My Business Supporters and Friends: I am very thankful my Inner Circle Group. Duke Williams has provided conversations that are always insightful, Ross Dik helped me think through the 14 Growth Principles, and Kurt Huffman and Mark Parrish took the time to review and provide great feedback and encouraged me to "Go, man, go!" Thank you to the many people who sat in my presentations as I was testing out these ideas.

A special thank you to Michael Hyatt for being willing to write the Foreword and for the team at Michael Hyatt and Co.: Joel and Megan Miller (Joel, I hope you know how much I appreciate your support), Chad Cannon, Deidra Romero, and the rest of their extraordinary team.

Michael Hyatt's BusinessAccelerator™ program provided me with a framework to stay focused on my goal, even through the interminably long "messy middle." A big thank you to my fellow BusinessAccelerator friends who were especially encouraging.

My Friends who provided great feedback on the manuscript: Marji Ross (your insights were invaluable), Debbie Dunham, and Susie Miller.

My Publisher: Morgan James Publishing. Founder, David Hancock (thanks for the title), Karen Anderson (yes, my wife and Associate Publisher), Jim Howard, and Margo Toulouse, Bethany Marshall,

Nickcole Watkins and all those on the Morgan James staff. Thank you for your encouragement and commitment to publishing a book that best represents my message.

My Editor/Writer and Friend: Nick Pavlidis is a man of many talents and skills. As a writer, attorney, and entrepreneur, he caught the vision for this book early on and has helped me bring that vision to life. His abilities have helped this book be clear, helpful, and interesting. Thank you, Nick, for all you did to make this book a reality. And thanks to Jennifer Harshman for expert editing and proofreading work. With so many moving parts involved in this project, your expertise and attention to detail have been priceless.

My Right-Hand Person: Sissi Haner sits behind her keyboard and is the tech genius behind all I do. She's brilliant, responsible, and has an uncanny attention to detail. She has been my "back office" for many years, and I couldn't do what I do without her. Her contribution to this book and my career is immeasurable.

Finally, my Book Coach: Besides being my wife, Karen is my co-writer, editor, publisher, and book coach (I've traded out by making her a lot of dinners!). She's done for me what she's done for countless authors—she's helped bring their books to life and made them readable, approachable, and more effective at communicating. Needless to say, I highly recommend her. (StrategicBookCoach.com). Thanks, honey, for all you've done to turn my dream into a reality.

I've been fortunate to have many dear friends. And if I haven't mentioned you by name, you are no less valuable to me, and I am grateful for you.

Again, my deepest thanks to all. Here's to changing the world and growing businesses everywhere like Amazon.

About the Authors

Steve Anderson, M.A., is a trusted authority on Risk, Technology, Productivity, and Innovation and has over thirty-five years of experience in the insurance industry. He holds a master's degree in Insurance Law.

Anderson is a professional speaker, consultant, and "futurist." His speaking portfolio includes presentations on the future of technology, how businesses can leverage the online world, and how any business can assess and use strategic risk to their advantage. He was chosen as one of the original 150 LinkedIn Influencers and has over 340,000 followers. To contact Steve, email Steve@ TheBezosLetters.com

Karen Anderson, M.S., is an author, publisher, and direct response marketer whose fingerprints are all over *New York Times, USA Today*, and other bestselling books. For the past 30+ years, she's helped entrepreneurs and businesses clarify and communicate their messages, grow their businesses, and increase

their reach using the power of a book. She grew up as an "insurance brat" and spent weekends with her dad looking behind buildings and parking lots checking for potential risks. To contact Karen, email Karen@TheBezosLetters.com

Steve and Karen have been married since 1975. They have two married daughters, but maybe more importantly, they have seven amazing young grandchildren and can't help but wonder if one (or more) of them may end up going into space.

They live in historic downtown Franklin, Tennessee.

Which of the "Anderson 14 Growth Principles" Does Your Business Need to Apply Today?

Start applying the 14 Growth Principles by taking the **free Anderson Risk Growth Assessment™**

- Gain powerful insights into where your company is *right now* with each principle.

- Discover which principle you should focus your resources on *first* for the biggest impact.

- Create a vision for risk and growth to *propel your company* to the next level.

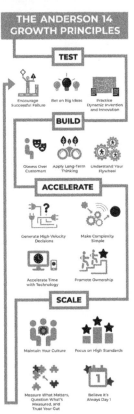

Endnotes

1   "2010 Baccalaureate Remarks." Princeton University. Accessed April 30, 2019. https://www.princeton.edu/news/2010/05/30/2010-baccalaureate-remarks.

2   "Annual Reports, Proxies and Shareholder Letters." Accessed March 1, 2019. https://ir.aboutamazon.com/annual-reports.

3   "AWS Culture." Amazon. Accessed March 1, 2019. https://aws.amazon.com/careers/culture/.

4   "Leadership Principles." Amazon. Accessed March 1, 2019. https://www.amazon.jobs/en/principles.

5   Blodget, Henry. "I Asked Jeff Bezos The Tough Questions—No Profits, The Book Controversies, The Phone Flop—And He Showed Why Amazon Is Such A Huge Success." *Business Insider*. December 13, 2014. Accessed April 30, 2019. https://www.businessinsider.com/amazons-jeff-bezos-on-profits-failure-succession-big-bets-2014-12.

6   Kranz, Gene. *Failure Is Not an Option: Mission Control from Mercury to Apollo 13 and Beyond*. New York: Simon & Schuster Paperbacks, 2009.

7   Hosking, Julie. "The Men Behind the Moon Landings." The West Australian. May 05, 2018. Accessed April 30, 2019. https://thewest.com.au/entertainment/theatre/to-the-moon-and-back-ng-b88796060z.

8   Blodget, Henry. "I Asked Jeff Bezos The Tough Questions—No

Profits, The Book Controversies, The Phone Flop—And He Showed Why Amazon Is Such A Huge Success."

9   "The David Rubenstein Show: Jeff Bezos." Bloomberg.com. September 19, 2018. Accessed April 30, 2019. https://www. bloomberg.com/news/videos/2018-09-19/the-david-rubenstein-show-jeff-bezos-video.

10 "Amazon Lab126." Amazon.jobs. Accessed April 30, 2019. https:// amazon.jobs/en/teams/lab126.

11 DeGeurin, Mack. "From Online Books to Smart Speaker Behemoth: How Amazon Conquered the Bookstore and is Using it to Showcase What's Next." Medium. October 11, 2018. Accessed April 30, 2019. https://medium.com/predict/from-bookstore-to-smart-speaker-behemoth-how-amazon-conquered-the-bookstore-and-is-using-it-to-2f73e6eb10bf.

12 "Amazon.com Introduces New Logo; New Design Communicates Customer Satisfaction and A-to-Z Selection." Amazon.com, Inc. Press Room. January 25, 2000. Accessed April 30, 2019. https:// press.aboutamazon.com/news-releases/news-release-details/ amazoncom-introduces-new-logo-new-design-communicates-customer.

13 Blodget, Henry. "Just the Latest Example of Why Amazon Is One of the Most Successful Companies in the World." Business Insider. December 09, 2012. Accessed April 30, 2019. https://www. businessinsider.com/why-amazon-is-one-of-the-most-successful-companies-in-the-world-2012-12.

14 Brand, Stewart. "About Long Now." The Long Now Foundation. Accessed April 30, 2019. http://longnow.org/about/.

15 "The 10,000 Year Clock." The Long Now Foundation. Accessed April 30, 2019. http://longnow.org/clock/.

16 Ibid.

17 Tweney, Dylan. "How to Make a Clock Run for 10,000 Years."

Wired. June 23, 2011. Accessed April 30, 2019. https://www.wired.com/2011/06/10000-year-clock/.

18 Stoll, John D. "For Companies, It Can Be Hard to Think Long Term." *The Wall Street Journal.* December 03, 2018. Accessed April 30, 2019. https://www.wsj.com/articles/for-companies-it-can-be-hard-to-think-long-term-1543846491.

19 "Market Caps of S&P 500 Companies 1979 - 2019." SiblisResearch.com. April 03, 2019. Accessed April 30, 2019. http://siblisresearch.com/data/market-caps-sp-100-us/.

20 Haden, Jeff. "Best From the Brightest: Jim Collins's Flywheel." Inc.com. January 21, 2014. Accessed April 30, 2019. https://www.inc.com/jeff-haden/the-best-from-the-brightest-jim-collins-flywheel.html.

21 Griswold, Alison. "Amazon Just Explained How Whole Foods Fits into Its Plan for World Domination." Quartz. July 30, 2018. Accessed April 30, 2019. https://qz.com/1113795/amazon-amzn-just-explained-how-whole-foods-fits-into-its-plan-for-world-domination/.

22 Collins, Jim. "Turning the Flywheel." Jim Collins - Books - Turning the Flywheel. January 2019. Accessed April 30, 2019. https://www.jimcollins.com/books/turning-the-flywheel.html.

23 "A Conversation with Jeff Bezos." Forum on Leadership. Accessed April 30, 2019. https://www.bushcenter.org/takeover/sessions/forum-leadership/bezos-closing-conversation.html.

24 Porter, Brad. "The Beauty of Amazon's 6-Pager." LinkedIn. Accessed April 30, 2019. https://www.linkedin.com/pulse/beauty-amazons-6-pager-brad-porter.

25 Rogers, Everett M. *Diffusion of Innovations.* 5th ed. New York: Free Press, 2003.

26 Ciolli, Joe. "Amazon's $1 Billion Purchase of PillPack Wiped out 15 times That from Pharmacy Stocks—and It Shows the Outsize Effect

the Juggernaut Can Have on an Industry." *Business Insider.* June 28, 2018. Accessed April 30, 2019. https://www.businessinsider.com/amazon-pharmacy-pillpack-acquisition-merger-showing-outsized-impact-2018-6.

27 "Amazon Fulfillment: FAQs." Accessed May 01, 2019. https://www.aboutamazon.com/amazon-fulfillment/faqs#how-many-fulfillment-and-sortation-centers-are-there-globally.

28 *Amazon Restricted Stock Units: Becoming an Owner. Amazon.* Accessed April 30, 2019. https://docplayer.net/8162546-Amazon-restricted-stock-units.html.

29 Roth, Daniel. "Top Companies 2019: Where the U.S. Wants to Work Now." LinkedIn. April 3, 2019. Accessed April 30, 2019. https://www.linkedin.com/pulse/top-companies-2019-where-us-wants-work-now-daniel-roth/.

30 "Leadership Principles." Amazon.

31 Day One Staff. "How to Build Your Own Amazon Door Desk." *The Amazon Blog: Day One* (blog), January 16, 2018. Accessed April 30, 2019. https://blog.aboutamazon.com/working-at-amazon/how-to-build-your-own-amazon-door-desk.

32 Karlinsky, Neal, and Jordan Stead. "How a Door Became a Desk, and a Symbol of Amazon." *The Amazon Blog: Day One* (blog), January 17, 2018. Accessed April 30, 2019. https://blog.aboutamazon.com/working-at-amazon/how-a-door-became-a-desk-and-a-symbol-of-amazon.

33 "The Jeff Bezos of 1999: Nerd of the Amazon." Interview by Bob Simon. CBS News. January 18, 2018. Accessed April 30, 2019. https://www.cbsnews.com/video/the-jeff-bezos-of-1999-nerd-of-the-amazon/

34 Yarow, Jay. "What It's Like Walking Around Amazon's Massive Offices In Seattle." *Business Insider.* June 24, 2013. Accessed April 30, 2019. https://www.businessinsider.com/what-its-like-walking-

around-amazons-massive-offices-in-seattle-2013-6.

35 "In-person Interview." Amazon.jobs. Accessed April 30, 2019.
    https://www.amazon.jobs/en/landing_pages/in-person-interview.

36 "Amazon Logistics." Amazon. Accessed April 30, 2019. https://
    logistics.amazon.com/marketing/opportunity.

37 "Drive with Uber—Make Money on Your Schedule." Uber.com.
    Accessed April 30, 2019. https://www.uber.com/us/en/drive/.

38 "Driving with Lyft Is Now Better than Ever." Lyft, Inc. Accessed
    April 30, 2019. https://www.lyft.com/driver/why-drive-with-lyft.

39 "Standards for Brands Selling in the Amazon Store." Amazon.
    Accessed April 30, 2019. https://sellercentral.amazon.com/gp/help/
    external/G201797950.

40 "Amazon Experimentation & Optimization." Amazon.jobs.
    Accessed April 30, 2019. http://www.amazon.jobs/en/teams/aeo.

41 "Jeff Bezos Reveals What It's like to Build an Empire and Become
    the Richest Man in the World—and Why He's Willing to Spend
    $1 Billion a Year to Fund the Most Important Mission of His
    Life." Interview by Mathias Döpfner. *Business Insider.* April 28,
    2018. Accessed April 30, 2019. https://www.businessinsider.com/
    jeff-bezos-interview-axel-springer-ceo-amazon-trump-blue-origin-
    family-regulation-washington-post-2018-4.

42 Lane, Randall. "Bezos Unbound: Exclusive Interview With The
    Amazon Founder On What He Plans To Conquer Next." *Forbes.*
    February 21, 2019. Accessed May 03, 2019. https://www.forbes.
    com/sites/randalllane/2018/08/30/bezos-unbound-exclusive-
    interview-with-the-amazon-founder-on-what-he-plans-to-conquer-
    next/.

43 "Jeff Bezos: Lake Forest Speech." C-SPAN.org. Accessed April 30,
    2019. https://www.c-span.org/video/?c4620829/jeff-bezos.

44 Davenport, Christian. *Space Barons: Elon Musk, Jeff Bezos, and the
    Quest to Colonize the Cosmos.* Thorndike Press, 2018.

45 Bechtel, Wyatt. "World's Richest Man Learned Work Ethic as a Kid on a Cattle Ranch." Drovers. May 22, 2018. Accessed April 30, 2019. http://www.drovers.com/article/worlds-richest-man-learned-work-ethic-kid-cattle-ranch.

46 Ibid.

47 "Jeffrey P. Bezos on Passion." Academy of Achievement: Keys to Success. Accessed April 30, 2019. https://www.achievement.org/video/bez0-pas-005/.

48 Digital image. Miami Herald Online Store. March 2, 2011. Accessed April 30, 2019. http://miamiheraldstore.mycapture.com/mycapture/enlarge.asp?image=34796019&event=1197554&CategoryID=58651.

49 "Brought to Book." Interview by Andrew Smith. *The Guardian.* February 10, 2011. Accessed April 30, 2019. https://www.theguardian.com/books/2001/feb/11/computingandthenet.technology.

50 "Our Mission." Blue Origin. Accessed April 30, 2019. https://www.blueorigin.com/our-mission.

51 "Interview: Jeff Bezos Lays out Blue Origin's Space Vision, from Tourism to Off-planet Heavy Industry." Interview by Alan Boyle. April 13, 2016. Accessed April 30, 2019. https://www.geekwire.com/2016/interview-jeff-bezos/.

52 "Our Mission." Blue Origin.

Recommended Books

Brandt, Richard L. *One Click: Jeff Bezos and the Rise of Amazon.com.* Portfolio/Penguin, 2012.

Collins, Jim. *Good to Great.* HarperCollins, 2001.

Collins, Jim. *Turning the Flywheel.* HarperCollins, 2019.

Davenport, Christian. *The Space Barons: Elon Musk, Jeff Bezos, and the Quest to Colonize the Cosmos.* PublicAffairs, 2018.

Galloway, Scott. *The Four.* Penguin, 2017.

Hunt, Helena. *First Mover: Jeff Bezos In His Own Words.* Agate B2, 2018.

Kranz, Gene. *Failure Is Not an Option.* Simon & Schuster, 2009.

MacGregor, JR. *Jeff Bezos: The Force Behind the Brand.* CAC Publishing LLC, 2018.

Piscione, Deborah Perry. *The Risk Factor.* St. Martin's Press, 2014.

Rossman, John. *The Amazon Way on IoT.* Clyde Hill Publishing, 2016.

Rossman, John. *Think Like Amazon: 50 1/2 Ideas to Become a Digital Leader.* McGraw-Hill Education, 2019.

Stone, Brad. *The Everything Store.* Little, Brown and Company, 2013.

Taleb, Nassim Nicholas. *The Black Swan.* Random House Trade Paperbacks, 2010.

Walton, Sam, and John Huey. *Sam Walton, Made in America.* Bantam Books, 1993.